FOR THE RECORD

THE STRUGGLE AND ULTIMATE POLITICAL RISE OF AMERICAN RECORDING MUSICIANS WITHIN THEIR LABOR MOVEMENT

Jon Burlingame

Foreword by *ED ASNER*

RECORDING MUSICIANS ASSOCIATION
HOLLYWOOD, CALIFORNIA

FOR THE RECORD

Copyright ©1997 Recording Musicians Association (RMA), all rights reserved. Except for brief quotations embodied in critical articles or reviews or as otherwise provided by law, this book may not be reproduced, transmitted, stored or retrieved in whole or in part, in any form or by any means now known to exist or yet to be invented, including, but not limited to, photocopying, scanning, recording or downloading without the express written permission from the copyright owner.

Printed in the United States of America

First printing June 1997

Published by the Recording Musicians Association (RMA)
817 Vine Street, Suite 209
Hollywood, California 90038-3715

Library Of Congress Catalog Number 97-68160

ISBN 0-9658464-0-7

DEDICATION

This book is dedicated to the unfailing and courageous spirit of the American recording musician. As consummate professionals, their talents are unknowingly appreciated on a daily basis by audiences worldwide.

𝄎

"...They are truly among the greatest contributors to our country's artistic life and are a cherished resource in which we can all take great pride."

–John Williams

CONTENTS

Publisher's Acknowledgments .... *vii*
Foreward by Edward Asner .... *ix*
Introduction by David Ewart .... *xiii*
Author's Acknowledgments .... *xvii*

The Musicians Guild of America 1

The First Recording Musicians Association
    Is Organized 33

The Tuesday Deal Spurs A National Alliance 47

Conference Status, Conflict In L.A.,
    And Growth Internationally 67

The RMA Today 89

Bibliography And Note On Sources *103*
About The Author *105*

PUBLISHER'S ACKNOWLEDGMENTS

The Recording Musicians Association gratefully acknowledges the generosity of Professional Musicians Local 47 (Los Angeles) in making the publication of this book a reality.

RMA also wishes to thank the following organizations and individuals for generously contributing to this project:

Local 802, New York
Local 10-208, Chicago
Local 149, Toronto
Local 257, Nashville
Local 105, Spokane
Local 389, Orlando
Local 153, San Jose

Cover photos and others: Laura Peterson
Assistant to Mr. Burlingame: Pam Gates
Computer layout, design and expertise: Laddie Chapman
Editors: David Ewart, Jay Berliner, Michael Comins
Project Coordinator: David Ewart

FOREWARD

by Edward Asner

When haven't we hummed a picture home? When doesn't the music live with us? People really don't know what goes into music in film and how its presence (and then its absence) convey moods, suggestions, that lead us along the way to the conclusion the director or producer wishes. The music of movies and television are a vital part, and a memorable part, of the American music scene. And there would be no music if there were no players.

The American Federation of Musicians represents those players, and other recording musicians throughout the United States and Canada. But the AFM hasn't always been responsive to the needs of the professional musician, and on several occasions over the past fifty years, uprisings have occurred within the rank and file that have forced the AFM to work harder on behalf of this small but vital segment of the membership.

Within all labor unions, you occasionally have independent movements, rebellions, primarily from whatever part of the membership – and it's usually the rank and file – who feel that their voices aren't being heard.

In 1972 I belonged to an independent movement that was trying to get multiple choices for candidates for office in the Screen Actors Guild, even proposing several choices as an official slate. It went nowhere at the time, but eventually it amassed enough power to elect Dennis Weaver as president, and slowly, more board members. So it took root and eventually led to my election, and that of Patty Duke, and a number of others.

An independent movement – no matter what a pain it can be at the time to an incumbent who thinks he's trying to do the best he can for the members – still serves the best interests of the union.

FOR THE RECORD

Artists have an innate tendency not to think of themselves as unionists, because to them that means a laboring man. It's an ancient prejudice and it has taken a long time to bury. If it wasn't for white-collar workers right now, unionism would be dead. But the effort must constantly be made. When a johnny-come-lately comes in and asks questions that were answered 40 or 50 years ago, you have to explain to him why those questions were answered that way.

It's very hard for an incumbent or an ongoing committee member to go through this time and again, but when that patience is given, the seedbed for new thoughts and new blood is laid. It can be time-consuming. But in the end those are the feet that march for you, and in marching for you, if you are fortunate enough to have some "names" at the top, then you'll present the solidarity that you so need to make an action viable.

The rank and file have produced the engineers who sweat and slave and finally arrive at the algebra by which our negotiators, our officers and our execs can go into contract negotiations and be able to present reasonable demands backed by logic and facts and figures. Without that rank and file this would not happen.

When we were on strike in 1980 and I was the star of a TV show, I attempted to support the musicians' action at that time as well. Our strike was finally settled, and we were faced with musicians picketing CBS/MTM studios where we filmed. Finally, it came time for me to go to work or be sued for breach of contract. I came to work, and when the musicians appearing in front of the studio gates saw me, they put down their picket signs and waved me into the studio. I am grateful to the union and its people, who were on strike far longer than us. I will forever be in their debt.

Edward Asner
May 15, 1997

Foreward

Edward Asner is a seven-time Emmy Award-winning actor. His long-running role as Lou Grant, first as the gruff but lovable TV news producer on "The Mary Tyler Moore Show" and later as the city editor of a Los Angeles newspaper on "Lou Grant," earned him five Emmys; his dramatically charged performances in "Roots" and "Rich Man, Poor Man" brought him two more. He has also received five Golden Globe Awards and was inducted into the Television Academy Hall of Fame in 1996. Asner served as National President of the Screen Actors Guild for two terms (1981-85).

INTRODUCTION

by David Ewart

Our story begins with the long post-World War II road of neglect recording musicians endured from their own American Federation of Musicians (AFM) causing them to secede and form their own guild, The Musicians Guild of America. This precipitated AFM compromises which ultimately brought them back into the union fold in 1962. Regrettably, the cycle of abuses continued forcing recording musicians to reorganize in 1969 as the Recording Musicians Association (RMA) to carry on their struggle for self-determination within the AFM.

While the Guild laid important political groundwork for recording musicians to gain control in matters affecting their livelihood, it was the RMA's many accomplishments as an advocacy organization that has now made it among the most popular and powerful volunteer membership groups in the history of the American labor movement. This popularity which has led the vast majority of AFM recording musicians to revere the RMA, has not always had a similar effect on the AFM leadership that represents well over 100,000 full and part-time musicians. In fact, numerous AFM administrations have aggressively fought the RMA's existence, utilizing recording musicians' financial support while resisting their input. It is important to note that while recording musicians constitute only a small percentage of the entire AFM membership, they carry by far the heaviest tax burden in the form of AFM work dues. Since the AFM is the only guild without a work dues cap, the disparity is often severe; e.g., in Los Angeles, 10% of the members pay nearly 90% of the dues!

The struggle to achieve this representation these musicians rightly deserve within their union structure has been ongoing for several generations. Some of the key battles covered in this retrospective include: the Petrillo years which resulted in the formation of The Musicians Guild of America; disputes over the Pension Fund; the Motion Picture Strike; Tuesday Productions – the AFM's "sweetheart deal" which threatened the jingle business in New York, Los Angeles, Toronto and Chicago and which ultimately unseated an AFM President; musicians of Local 47 against its administration led by President Bernie Fleischer (including the aftermath of a multimillion dollar lawsuit by the deposed President); and the rejection of a Special Payments Fund work dues initiative sponsored by AFM leaders.

Many of the positive milestones achieved by recording musicians include: the formation of the Motion Picture and Phonograph Special Payments Funds; the addition of a rank-and-file player appointed to the AFM Negotiation Sub-Committee; RMA achieving AFM conference status; the creation of "Oversight Committees" to monitor the Special Payments Funds; the formation of The Joint Cooperative Committee; the appointment of a rank-and-file Pension Fund Trustee; and the celebration of the AFM's 100th birthday sponsored by the AFM Player Conference, ICSOM, OCSM, ROPA and RMA.

To ensure the veracity of this book, writer Jon Burlingame has drawn from pertinent, rare literary works, related news clippings, official journals of the AFM and its Locals, RMA newsletters, and most importantly, actual interviews with "history makers" themselves.

The reader will witness many first-hand accounts of historical events by leading professional musicians who were there. Regrettably, some of the participants to have been interviewed are no longer with us. We thank all those interviewed for unselfishly donating their time and energies. An even deeper appreciation is extended to the many volunteer representatives chronicled in this book such as RMA President Dennis Dreith. Undeniably, there would have been no basis for this remarkable movement without the steadfast vision and integrity of Cecil Read, the founder of The Musicians Guild of America. It is such charismatic leaders and the many devoted followers who exemplify the legendary spirit of this political movement most vividly.

RMA sincerely thanks the many "unsung heroes" who participated in this political process. It is important to recognize that those included in this book are representative of the great many numbers who served this movement.

Finally, RMA thanks you, the reader, for the important role of judging this history, and for being a party to its impact upon our continuing music profession. *"Those who cannot remember the past are condemned to repeat it."* (George Santayana, 1863-1942)

AUTHOR'S ACKNOWLEDGMENTS

First of all, my thanks go to all of the people who agreed to be interviewed for this book. Many of them are legendary session players whose names I had read on the back covers of old LPs and whom I never expected to meet, much less interview about a crucial period in all of their lives. All were generous with their time and memories.

Three people associated with the Recording Musicians Association must be singled out, notably Dennis Dreith, the president of the organization whose knowledge, patience and good humor made a complex project just a bit easier; David Ewart, the RMA's editor and publisher, whose help in tracking down people and whose many constructive suggestions improved this chronicle in ways that, I hope, make it a worthwhile addition to the canon of works about American labor; and Jay Berliner, whose detailed records helped me to pinpoint elusive dates, people and places throughout this history.

Finally, a personal note. I have always been in awe of the studio musicians who play film, TV, and commercial music for a living. They are among the finest players in the world, and it's been my good fortune over the past several years to watch these people at work (often sight-reading very difficult music and playing it beautifully on the first rehearsal).

What I didn't know until I undertook this project was the degree of courage and commitment that many of them displayed, particularly during the Guild years. These people were already extraordinary by virtue of their talent. What they accomplished in the face of overwhelming negative reaction from within their own union makes them even more remarkable.

Jon Burlingame
May 1997

James Caesar Petrillo, International AFM President, 1940-1958

THE MUSICIANS GUILD OF AMERICA

Why It Happened And What It Did

In the 1940s and '50s, the American Federation of Musicians was very different than the AFM of today. Union musicians were virtually penalized for being busy with film, radio, television and recording dates: the result of outdated, even legally questionable policies, and the outrageous tactics of longtime AFM president James Caesar Petrillo.

Petrillo became International president in 1940. A poorly educated, failed trumpet player, he was raised in the Chicago ghetto and became a union boss in the '20s. His "dese-dem-and-dose" speeches endeared him to tens of thousands of small-local AFM members – few of whom earned their living as musicians – who kept him in power.

Incredible as it seems today, Petrillo was opposed to the mechanical reproduction of music. "He lived in an era when there were pit bands," recalled studio trumpeter Uan Rasey, whose memorable solos graced many classic films ranging from *An American in Paris* to *Chinatown*. Rasey was one of the "rebels" of Los Angeles Local 47 who was expelled twice for his stance against Petrillo's policies. "He thought if we didn't record anything, he would bring the pit bands back."

FOR THE RECORD

Uan Rasey

An outspoken advocate of the performance of live music, Petrillo instituted a ban on all phonograph and transcription recordings in August 1942. Public and press were outraged, particularly when government officials suggested that Petrillo's ban was hindering the war effort. It lasted more than two years and was only lifted when the controversial union leader forced the record companies to "pay fixed royalties to the Federation for each record and transcription made."

The money was to be used to reduce unemployment among musicians (supposedly thrown out of work by the growing phonograph-record business) by providing free concerts of live music around the country. Initially called the Recording and Transcription Fund, it was modified into the Music Performance Trust Fund (MPTF) after the Taft-Hartley Act became law in 1947 and another Petrillo ban on recordings took place during most of 1948.

The trust fund grew by millions of dollars every year. By the early 1950s it was receiving payments from record companies, movie producers (for the sale of their films to TV) and producers of jingles and filmed television shows. In fact, the growing popularity of the new television medium became a crucial factor in the revolt that was then beginning to brew among musicians in Los Angeles and, to a lesser degree, New York.

Petrillo, still waging war on all types of recorded music, in 1951 negotiated an agreement with the four major networks that called for a payment by every producer who wanted to use AFM musicians for recording a television score. The amount was 5 percent of the show's overall budget.

"Let's say, in those days, you had a half-hour television film with a budget of $50,000," explained trombonist Lloyd Ulyate, another of the Local 47 rebels. "You'd have to pay $2,500 into the trust fund before you even could hire a musician."

A handful of Hollywood producers agreed to the demand: the makers of "I Love Lucy," "The Loretta Young Show," "Dragnet"

Lloyd Ulyate

and "Medic," for example. The vast majority, however, balked at this massive financial obligation and began buying and/or building "track libraries" consisting of music that was often written in L.A. but recorded in foreign countries (mostly England, Germany, and Mexico). CBS music director Lud Gluskin, for example, went abroad every year, recording hundreds of hours of music that could be used again and again on filmed shows without paying a dime to American musicians or the trust fund.

Vince DiBari, former AFM Executive Board Member and Local 47 Vice President

In the case of "I Love Lucy," Desi Arnaz actually flew back to New York to meet with Petrillo on the issue. Vince DiBari, who played second trumpet in the band and who later became vice president of Local 47, was one of five musicians who accompanied Arnaz on the 1952 trip. The players weren't allowed into the meeting, but upon leaving Petrillo's office, DiBari said, "Desi called him every name under the sun in Spanish." Petrillo didn't budge.

"The independents thought it was highway robbery," said Ulyate. "Not only that, they had to pay another $2,500 every time there was a rerun." By 1955, four-fifths of all filmed TV shows were being scored with so-called "canned music" recorded overseas.

Los Angeles musicians were losing an immense amount of work. Then, in June 1955, musicians who had worked on film scores lost their contractually negotiated $25 payment for every film sold to TV. That's when Petrillo and the AFM Executive Board directed movie companies to stop paying the individual musicians and instead make the payment to the trust fund. In nine months, according to one estimate, Los Angeles musicians lost $2.5 million that was owed to them.

Petrillo even went so far as to mandate that recording musicians, who had been granted a 10 percent wage hike in 1954 (from the $41.25 phonograph scale per three-hour session, and the first raise in eight years), would never see a dime of it. All of the increase was diverted into the Trust Fund.

How could Petrillo get away with this? Article 1, Section 1, of the Federation bylaws effectively gave the president dictatorial powers, making policy, altering rules or issuing any directives he felt appropriate. Press references to him as "Little Caesar," "U.S. music czar" and even "musical Hitler" were commonplace.

By late 1955, Los Angeles musicians were fed up. Alto sax player Phil Sobel, who was among the most militant of the dissidents, even confronted the union leader in person: "I said, 'Mr. Petrillo, you

FOR THE RECORD

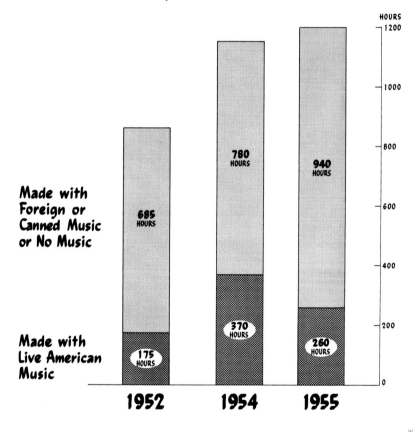

Phil Sobel

have taken the bread out of my kids' mouths. I don't like that. I don't want to give it to the trust fund before I get it for my family.'"

French horn player Vincent De Rosa tried to explain the issues to Petrillo at a meeting of Local 47's board of directors. He wasn't interested. Petrillo's parting words to De Rosa were: "Well, kid, cinch up your belt, 'cause it's gonna get a lot tougher."

The unrepentant Petrillo frequently referred to "those selfish Hollywood musicians" and "$800-a-week Communist fiddle players in Hollywood." In fact, numerous contemporary accounts written from a variety of viewpoints confirm that he used the trust fund and its dispersal of monies around the country as political patronage, keeping hundreds of small locals happy literally at the expense of the working musician.

A 1956 *Reader's Digest* article, entitled "The Union That Fights Its Workers," came right to the point: "Last year $2,080,000, with-

FOR THE RECORD

Vince De Rosa

held from the musicians who earned it, was dribbled into 654 areas in which the union's locals are located. The money was slivered among 179,000 beneficiaries, giving each an average $11.60 'unemployment benefit.'"

The story quoted Petrillo, at that year's annual AFM convention in Atlantic City, as castigating the Los Angeles crowd (which was there to protest his authoritarian policies). "When these fellows were pumpin' away and makin' the bucks, we created a trust fund and a new principle: givin' money to the non-employed," he said. The "non-employed" musicians were for the most part dentists, merchants, machinists – members who only occasionally picked up an instrument – and they roared with approval at Petrillo's words.

Justin Gordon (L) with Henry Mancini's sax section for the 1969 Academy Awards

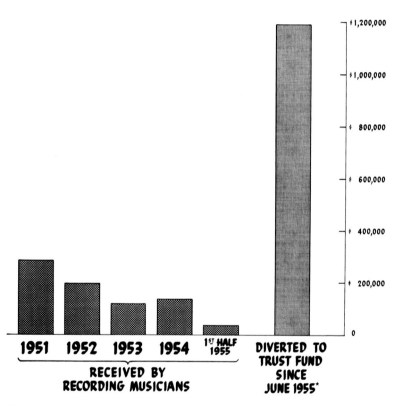

"The trust fund's stated aim was to promote live music," said saxophone player Justin Gordon, another Local 47 dissident. "It was distributed on a monthly or yearly basis to the many locals throughout the country. But it became a political slush fund. Occasionally they would play a live concert – if the town was big enough to have enough musicians. Otherwise, they just distributed it. Here's your money, and here's yours." The voting structure of the AFM ensured that the big locals (New York, Chicago, Los Angeles, where the majority of professional musicians lived and worked) would always be voted down by the dozens of small locals that remained in Petrillo's pocket.

In addition, "the recording musician had no pensions, no royalties, no reuse payments and no right of ratification of any contracts," sax player Ted Nash recalled. "We were not even allowed to have a committee to express our needs prior to any upcoming contract negotiations." Another gripe: Petrillo had diverted $275,000 from the Trust Fund into a pension fund that served only top union officials and their dependents.

A handful of Los Angeles musicians, among them the top players for film, TV and recordings, fomented a very public revolt against Petrillo and his policies in 1956. Leading the group was Cecil F. Read, then 46, characterized by *The Los Angeles Times* as "soft-spoken but dynamic." Read had played first trumpet on the film soundtrack of *Oklahoma!*, on TV's "Loretta Young Show" and on recordings by such vocalists as Gordon MacRae and Mario Lanza. He was vice president of Local 47.

Wrote *The Times*: "No one could look or act less like a labor politician than Read. Of medium height, well dressed, with trimmed, graying mustache, he presents the outward appearance of a prosperous businessman. In fact, he is one of the highest-paid and professionally respected first trumpets in Hollywood's dog-eat-dog competition within the entertainment world."

Read was also a very religious man, a Christian Scientist, according to his surviving colleagues. "Cecil was a very highly principled man," recalled Ulyate. "When he saw this injustice, he took it upon himself to be the leader. He gave up playing. He gave his life to this, and without his leadership, [the revolt] never would have happened." Added Nash: "Cecil was a brilliant guy. He could

Cecil Read, Ted Nash and Justin Gordon

size up the situation and put his finger right on the pulse of it. Plus, he had very high morals. He was a guy that everyone looked up to. He came to the front when we needed somebody."

The arbitrary rerouting of the $25-per-film payment was the last straw for recording musicians. In September 1955, the membership of Local 47 voted to formally appeal this action and Trust Fund

Ted Nash

policy in general, and in January 1956, Read met with Petrillo and the International Executive Board in New York City to plead the case. The effort was futile.

At that meeting, Read later recalled, "I was subjected to the 'Petrillo technique' for about an hour. Pounding on the table, yelling and blustering, [about] what a great man he was, how much he had done, how much the musicians owed him, et cetera. At the end of a lengthy tirade about how he had fought for the Trust Fund principle, he stated, 'I would kill before I would let anyone touch that fund.' Then he added, after he realized what he said, 'And I'm not a killing man.'"

(Rumors abounded about Petrillo's Old-Chicago-style tactics. More than one musician reported seeing Petrillo settle disputes by pulling out a concealed gun and placing it carefully on the table before him, a not-so-veiled threat of possible violence if his demands weren't met. Although he was the subject of Congressional investigation on several occasions, he was never formally charged with any crime. But he was feared.)

The rank-and-file action that would change the entire course of the American Federation of Musicians began on February 27, 1956.

Cecil Read elected officer of Local 47 (being congratulated by Felix Slatkin)

Richard Perrisi at ousting of Local 47 President John TeGroen

An estimated 2,800 members of Local 47 met at the Hollywood Palladium to shout then-president John TeGroen out of office and replace him with Cecil Read. TeGroen was perceived as a Petrillo puppet, Read the man who could lead the AFM's second-largest local (16,500 of the total of 260,000 members) against one of the nation's most powerful union bosses.

At that meeting, Read denounced Petrillo and his manipulation of the $14-million Trust Fund as his "personal political slush fund to perpetuate himself in office." Said Read: "We can submit to these injustices and let Petrillo and company continue to rub our noses in the dirt. Or we can assert our right as free American citizens to break this immoral dictatorship with which we have been shackled."

The story made headlines. "L.A. Musicians Revolt Over Petrillo" read the banner in the next day's *Los Angeles Times.* Over the next few months, *The New York Times, Daily Variety, The Nation, Saturday Review, Down Beat, The Wall Street Journal,* and dozens of other publications would report the issues. Petrillo, already a favorite target of the press for his recording bans of the '40s, would be increasingly vilified as a dangerously powerful demagogue out of step with the times.

But Local 47 was by no means unified on the issues. Hundreds agreed that the time was right for a break with Petrillo, but many also felt that to defy the national leadership was disloyal, even anti-union; still others waited to see the way the winds were blowing, feeling that their best bet was to side with those who looked like the winners in the long run.

And the battle, dissidents knew, would not be cheap. Legal counsel was already necessary, and the prospect of fighting a protracted court fight with the AFM was daunting. So the group came up with a novel idea. As Gordon explained it: "Whenever we were on a record date or a studio call or anything involved in these fields that we were concerned with, we would pass an envelope around and have each guy throw a buck in the envelope."

A handful of artists sided with the maligned musicians. A Frank Sinatra date provided a memorable example, Gordon said. "Sinatra watched it going around. It finally came back to me. He came over, and he said, 'Let me see the envelope.' I said, 'Okay, Frank, here you are.' He reached into his pocket and stuffed something into the envelope. And I said, 'Thanks a lot.' I opened up the envelope: it was a hundred-dollar bill." Ultimately, according to Rasey, the group raised $260,000 to support their fight.

Petrillo, whose power had never been so publicly challenged, immediately mobilized his forces against the rebel faction. Famed labor lawyer Henry Kaiser was AFM's chief counsel, and ex-CIO general counsel Arthur J. Goldberg (later President John F. Kennedy's Secretary of Labor and still later a Supreme Court Justice) was named referee for the subsequent "trial" of Read and 12 of his strongest supporters.

Their expulsion from the union was upheld in sensational fashion at the June 1956 AFM convention in Atlantic City, N.J., where a day-long debate on the issues was capped by the public airing of a tape recording that had secretly been made at a meeting of Read and his followers. Read could be heard calling Petrillo a "dictator" and outlining plans for fighting him in the courts and through the National Labor Relations Board.

Read, solidly backed by the majority of active members in Local 47, continued to lead the rebels despite his "official" displacement as vice president. Over the next year, they filed four lawsuits against the Federation – alleging damages of more than $15 million – which effectively stopped all re-use and royalty payments into the Trust Fund by film producers, TV distributors and record companies. (Eventually all four were settled to the tune of about $3.5 million, with the courts agreeing that the wage increases should be returned to the players, not left in the trust fund.)

At one point, a West Coast contingent flew to New York to seek support from Local 802 musicians. According to trumpeter-composer Murray Rothstein, "support was overwhelming" but 802 President Al Manuti ruled the vote out of order and adjourned the meeting for "lack of decorum." More than 1,000 outraged members later held an unofficial, late-night meeting, electing a steering committee that eventually developed into the Unison Club that worked to rid 802 of the corrupt Manuti administration. Manuti personally warned members to "stay away" from the Guild.

As 1958 began, the AFM was negotiating for a new contract with the major motion-picture studios. When talks broke down in February, the Federation called a strike and 300 contract musicians in the studio orchestras (along with arrangers, copyists and librarians) walked out of Allied Artists, Columbia, Walt Disney Productions, MGM, Warner Bros., Paramount, 20th Century-Fox and Universal.

Cecil Read elected President, Musicians Guild of America, 1958

Now, in the view of the insurgents, Hollywood musicians were not only being deprived of income that was rightfully theirs (the $25 per film payments, the wage hike being diverted into the Trust Fund, the work lost because of European-produced soundtracks for TV film caused by Petrillo's 5 percent tax on producers), but they couldn't work at all.

Read and company saw no alternative. In March 1958, while the strike was on, they decided to leave the AFM and form their own group: the Musicians Guild of America. "To us," explained Gordon, "union was a dirty word, only because of the way our union was functioning. None of us were anti-union. But the union must work for you, and [the AFM] did everything *but* work for us; they worked against us."

The formation of the MGA, or the Guild as it became known, divided the membership of Local 47. Working through legal channels to redress grievances was one thing; "dual unionism," the bane of organized labor through the years, was something else entirely and forced hundreds of loyal union members to make a choice.

"Cecil Read felt that things were not happening fast enough, and he decided to form his own union," recalled Max Herman, who later became president of Local 47. "I did not believe that that was the way to go. We all wanted the same things, but he felt that it was not going to happen unless there was another union. It was a very unhappy situation. Friends of 30 and 40 years didn't talk to each other," Herman said. While Herman supported Read's aims (and had, in fact, managed Read's initial campaign for vice president), he remained in Local 47 and did not join the Guild.

Another musician who did not support the secessionist forces was Marl Young, a nightclub and rehearsal pianist who later became composer of "The Lucy Show" (and had been instrumental in the 1953 amalgamation of the black Los Angeles Local 767 and white Local 47). The first black board member of Local 47, he attended

Max Herman, President of Local 47, 1972-1983, 1991-1992

many of Cecil Read's early meetings and opposed the suspension of pro-Guild members. "But I was strictly on the side of the union," he said. "It's hard enough when you've got everybody together; when you split, the employers can just murder you."

Stated Ted Nash: "We were never proud of our role as a splinter group in a dual-unionism environment, but it was the only way that the survival of the recording musician could be attained."

Petrillo's day was over. His failure to crush the opposition to his reactionary policies; the mishandled negotiations with the film producers, including an ill-advised strike; and the threat to the AFM that the Guild now posed, led him to announce his retirement in May 1958 after 18 years as all-powerful music czar. The torch was passed to Herman D. Kenin, who as AFM West Coast representative had been deeply involved in negotiations with the dissidents of Local 47 and knew the situation first-hand.

The Musicians Guild of America 21

The headline in the July 12, 1958 edition of *The Los Angeles Times* said it all: "Film Musicians Kick Out AFM, Support New Guild; Petrillo Group Meets Stunning Defeat in Vote." By a vote of 580 to 484 in a National Labor Relations Board-sanctioned election, the Musicians Guild of America wrested the right from the Federation to negotiate with the major studios. As the story pointed out, "Hollywood's professional musicians wrote a new chapter in labor

Marl Young, Local 47 Executive Board 1956-1960, 1973-1975, Secretary 1975-1982, Trustee 1990-1992

union history yesterday." An estimated 1,400 musicians were eligible to vote; nearly 1,200 did.

Read moved quickly to settle the 20-week strike and negotiate a contract with the studios.

"At our peak, the Guild had maybe 1,500 members," said Gordon. "However, the professionals – the guys that knew and understood what we were doing – were very much with us. I don't know to this day how we won it, but we won that election. It took us six weeks, but we sat down with the motion picture producers and negotiated a contract."

In its maiden effort, the Guild managed a breakthrough that the AFM could not. It received a guarantee from the studios that every filmed television series would have at least one recording session per 13 episodes. It was a bare minimum, to be sure, but the producers were happy to agree in exchange for being rid of Petrillo's prohibitively expensive 5 percent "tax" on filmed TV shows. "Don't think we didn't get criticized for that," recalled Gordon. "But we felt we're breaking into a new field, and it's got to pay off. Well, it ultimately did. After a while everybody was recording because it was so convenient."

Indeed, the immediate success of the Henry Mancini-scored "Peter Gunn" (which went on the air in September 1958) and a separate, AFM-negotiated agreement with Revue (which produced such popular shows as "Wagon Train" and "Alfred Hitchcock Presents") that guaranteed $2 million in wages for TV scoring, led to dozens of shows being scored on a regular basis in Los Angeles. Within the next two years, the "canned music" plague of cut-rate, foreign-made TV soundtracks was virtually eliminated.

Among other provisions in the Guild agreement, Nash pointed out: "[Performing for] theatrical film production would be on an individual, freelance basis operating within the economic-reality window of supply and demand, functioning to find its own level.

The Musicians Guild of America

Guild representation election, 1958

NLRB certification given to Camille, the Guild's only paid employee, 1958

(L-R) Ted Nash, Cecil and Dotty Read at Guild victory celebration dinner

Guild takes jurisdiction from AFM in motion picture field, 1958

All this, unfortunately, meant that the major studio staff orchestras had to go. We made a lot of enemies on that one, but time soothed all wounds."

Most importantly, the Guild principle of allowing musicians to ratify their own contracts (something that AFM officials had always deemed unimportant) was upheld. Predictably, the AFM criticized the Guild agreement as eliminating residuals and re-use payments, and abolishing contract orchestras – but the AFM, in its next contracts with the record industry, the TV networks, and the jingle business, began to incorporate Guild-originated provisions.

During the two years of the Guild's contract with the studios, Kenin abolished the dictatorial clause of Article 1, Section 1 of the AFM by-laws; eliminated the 5 percent tax on scoring for TV films; began reducing contributions to the Trust Fund; rerouted to musicians the 21 percent wage hike on records that had been going into the Fund; and, significantly, established a pension plan for casually employed musicians.

The AFM tried repeatedly to convince the NLRB to overturn the Guild's position as bargaining agent for studio players. A 1959 Kenin statement was typical, referring to "the problems created by the Musicians Guild of America in its sweetheart contract with the major studios which have been a threat to musicians everywhere."

In the next NLRB election, in September 1960, the AFM regained jurisdiction as collective bargaining agent for studio musicians. The vote was close, 473-408. The AFM win, due in no small measure because of its gradual adoption of Guild ideas, was a confirmation that the Guild had been right all along. Kenin, to his credit, moved toward reconciliation with this statement: "We regard the election results more as a reaffirmation of musicians' unity than as a victory over other musicians."

By November, the AFM had negotiated a strong new three-and-a-half-year contract with the studios, upping the mandatory TV scoring sessions from one to six for every 13 one-hour episodes, plus wage hikes and pension contributions.

Max Herman, who was then vice-president of Local 47, was among those who met with Kenin during the Guild years, explaining the problems that the Trust Fund controversy had caused and

Herman Kenin, AFM President 1958-1970

urging that fence-mending begin by diverting at least a part of the monies that rightfully belonged to the musicians.

The Guild continued its agreements with several TV producers and record companies, notably Sinatra's Reprise label. "In 1961, we decided we needed some help from New York," Gordon reported. "New York was a much bigger local, in the area of about 30,000 members at the time. Four of us went to New York. We spent two weeks there; we called everybody we knew and spread the word. Many of them were just so damned scared they wouldn't go near us. I can't substantiate some of the stories we heard, but we were told that the guys on staff at NBC were told that if they went anywhere near our hotel they would be fired. We got, roughly, 200 or 300 people that had the guts to at least talk to us." Unfortunately, only a handful agreed to join the Guild.

But the Guild contingent got a surprise: AFM chief counsel Henry Kaiser called and asked for a meeting. "We met with Henry at a small hotel on the East Side," Gordon recalled. "He said, 'Now look, guys. A lot of people are getting hurt. It's about time we end this thing.'"

Negotiations began, quietly, between the Guild and the AFM. "Kenin agreed with Cecil that on every national contract, there will be ratification by the people who do the work," recalled Max Herman. "The Trust Fund would stand," Ulyate added, "but half of that would become a Special Payments Fund. On phonograph records, a certain percentage of every sale went to this Trust Fund. The deal was, of the money that was paid in, half would go to the Trust Fund and half would go to the guys who made the record."

All of this took several months. As Kenin stated in his September 1961 letter to Read: "The fundamental premise and underlying theme of our discussions and of the understandings they produced was that the interest of professional musicians could best be promoted by the consolidation of their total economic and political power into a single union."

In his letter, Kenin formally agreed to alter the record contracts "so that 50 percent of the monies now payable to the Music Performance Trust Fund will be paid to the musicians who contribute to the making of the records." The AFM also agreed to "seek residual or reuse payments for the recording musician in all other recording fields."

All Guild members were reinstated as AFM members without penalty; musicians were to be given "the right to ratify all contracts"; and a Recording Musicians Advisory Committee was established starting in April 1962. This unit, comprised of musicians in various recording fields (film, TV, records, jingles, etc.), was designed to "advise and consult with the Federation respecting all matters affecting the interests of recording musicians [including] the formulation of bargaining demands," and participate in collective bargaining negotiations.

Read and most of his fellow dissidents – having achieved much of what they set out to do – agreed to the terms and the Guild was dissolved.

"We were more than glad to dissolve an organization that had done its job by securing a future for the recording musician," wrote Ted Nash. "The Guild founders were never intent on creating a permanent entity with the purpose of destroying a long-standing, viable institution as the AF of M. We merely wanted to break their stranglehold on our careers and establish a firm foothold for future recording musicians in this new age of electronic advances."

Guild members were unanimous in their praise and admiration for Cecil Read. "Throughout all this," said Nash, "Cecil was just a tower of strength and such a pleasure to work with. It was quite a sacrifice for him, because he was very successful [as a musician]. But this was his life, knowing that none of the rest of us were up to it. It helped our cause, knowing what he was giving up for it. He was just a fantastic guy. He made a lot of enemies because of the stand that he took. At the time, it was very unpopular to be a splinter, anti-union group, no matter what the cause."

If Read had quit, the entire movement would have collapsed, De Rosa believed. "Without him, we wouldn't have anything. It would have been over. What a wonderful man Cecil Read was. One of the finest men I've ever met in my life. Here's a guy who was at the top of his profession. He couldn't back out, nor did he ever say that he would. He never complained.

"People today don't understand," De Rosa added. "We would never have had pensions, residuals, anything like that."

Said Phil Sobel: "Everything we have now came from the Guild. That was the education of all musicians, the first they had ever had about the business they're in. A realistic look at how their business was run, worked, and what the obstacles are. They never knew it before."

AMERICAN FEDERATION OF MUSICIANS
OF THE UNITED STATES AND CANADA
AFFILIATED WITH THE A.F.L.-C.I.O.

REGISTERED

September 5, 1961

OFFICE OF THE PRESIDENT
425 Park Avenue
New York 22, N. Y.

INTERNATIONAL EXECUTIVE BOARD

HERMAN D. KENIN
President
425 Park Avenue
New York 22, N. Y.
Phone: PLaza 8-0600

WILLIAM J. HARRIS
Vice-President
418½ N. St. Paul Street
Dallas 1, Texas
Phone: Riverside 7-2889

STANLEY BALLARD
Secretary
220 Mt. Pleasant Avenue
Newark 4, N. J.
Phone: HUmboldt 4-6600

GEORGE V. CLANCY
Treasurer
220 Mt. Pleasant Avenue
Newark 4, N. J.
Phone: HUmboldt 4-6600

LEE REPP
2200 Carnegie Avenue
Cleveland 15, Ohio

E. E. "Joe" STOKES
5000 Polk Avenue
Houston 23, Texas

ALFRED J. MANUTI
261 West 52nd Street
New York 19, N. Y.

CHARLES H. KENNEDY
230 Jones Street
San Francisco 2, Calif.

WALTER M. MURDOCH
Rooms 545-546
17 Queen Street, East
Toronto 1, Ont., Canada

JAMES C. PETRILLO
Honorary President
175 West Washington St.
Chicago 2, Illinois

C. L. BAGLEY
Vice-President Emeritus
300 Continental Building
408 South Spring Street
Los Angeles 13, Calif.

LEO CLUESMANN
Secretary Emeritus
32 South Munn Avenue
East Orange, N. J.

J. W. PARKS
Honorary Executive
Board Member
502 North Denver Street
Dallas 3, Texas

Board of Directors
Musicians Guild of America
Suite 208 Equitable Building
6253 Hollywood Boulevard
Hollywood 28, California

Attention: <u>Mr. Cecil F. Read, President</u>

Gentlemen:

As you know, discussions have been going on for some months between representatives of the Guild and of the Federation looking toward the reunification of all musicians. These discussions have culminated in basic understandings reached by your President, Mr. Cecil F. Read and myself as President of the American Federation of Musicians, the substance of which I record in this letter.

Preliminarily, I want to express my personal and official thanks for the unfailing courtesy displayed by your representatives throughout the course of these conversations.

The fundamental premise and underlying theme of our discussions and of the understandings they produced was that the interest of professional musicians could best be promoted by the consolidation of their total economic and political power into a single union.

To achieve that vital unity, you agree to recommend the dissolution of the Musicians' Guild of America as soon as possible in reliance upon the Federation's agreement as follows:

1) <u>Reuse and Residual Payments</u>. The Federation will as soon as possible seek to negotiate a change in the existing phonograph record agreements so that 50% of the monies now payable to the Music Performance Trust Fund will be paid

American Federation of Musicians
PRESIDENT'S OFFICE

Board of Directors   September 5, 1961
Musicians Guild of America   Page Two
Att: Mr. Cecil F. Read, President

to the musicians who contribute to the making of the records. Additionally the Federation reaffirms its policy to seek residual or reuse payments for the recording musician in all other recording fields.

2) Ratification. Musicians who have been expelled from the Federation and Local #47 because of their support of the Guild or its activities, will be reinstated to membership in Local #47 and in the Federation with full, uninterrupted rights and privileges of such memberships (as though never expelled). All fines that have been imposed on musicians because of activities stemming from the existence and actions of the Guild shall be nullified; that is, those who have paid such fines (or new initiation fees because of such fines) shall be made whole, and those who have been suspended or expelled for non-payment of such fines shall be restored to membership in Local #47 and in the Federation with full uninterrupted rights and privileges of such memberships (as though never expelled).

3) Ratification. The Federation reaffirms its policy to grant to all musicians employed in the fields within the Federation's jurisdiction the right to ratify all contracts it negotiates.

4) Recording Musicians Advisory Committee. Not later than April 1, 1962 the Federation will cause to be established in Los Angeles a committee democratically selected at regular intervals by all members working in the recording field (phonograph records, motion picture film, TV film and tape, transcriptions, jingles and spots) in the Los Angeles area. Those serving as members of the committee must be actively working in the recording field during the time of such service. The committee shall include a representative of the arrangers (elected exclusively by arrangers)

American Federation of Musicians

PRESIDENT'S OFFICE

Board of Directors
Musicians Guild of America
Att: Mr. Cecil F. Read, President

September 5, 1961
Page Three

and a representative of copyists (elected exclusively by copyists). The committee shall have the right to communicate directly to the Federation its advice and opinions respecting all matters affecting the interests of recording musicians. It shall advise and consult with the Federation respecting the formulation of bargaining demands. Additionally, a representative or representatives of the committee shall serve in an advisory capacity at all Federation collective bargaining negotiations.

The International Executive Board of the Federation has already approved these understandings, and we hope that you and your membership will promptly do the same so that with the strength of unity we can all work together to realize our common objectives.

Sincerely,

[signature]
President

HDK:dm

THE FIRST RECORDING MUSICIANS ASSOCIATION IS ORGANIZED

The dissatisfaction of recording musicians with their treatment by the AFM manifested itself in many forms. Arranger Nick Perito recalled a 1960 meeting at New York's Palm Garden, attended by AFM president Herman Kenin and several other Federation officers. Referring to the imminent demise of the Musicians Guild, Kenin announced, "The Pied Piper in California has lost his tune."

An angry Perito, who had been a vocal supporter of Cecil Read and the Guild, took the podium to respond: "If he's lost his tune, none of you guys ever knew the chord changes. You gentlemen sitting on that stage are determining my destiny, yet none of you know what the inside of a recording studio even looks like, let alone performing or earning a living in it. You sit up there and determine what's going to happen with me, my economic life, and eventually the lives of my family."

The hundreds of New York musicians present responded enthusiastically to Perito's impassioned words, frequently interrupting with applause and offering a standing ovation when he finished. Kenin and company wisely chose not to engage in a public debate.

A few weeks later, Perito and about a dozen colleagues formed the Recording Musicians Society of New York, a loose-knit collection of leading players who met once a month in an effort to improve conditions for recording musicians in Local 802. One of Perito's early issues involved a lower scale for small record companies; 802 president Manuti accused Perito variously of being "a Communist, a rebel, and anti-American." The society made no real headway on issues and quietly disbanded a year or so later.

In Los Angeles, meanwhile, the agreement to dissolve the Guild enabled a group of Los Angeles musicians to begin advising the Federation on contract issues. Called the Los Angeles Recording Musicians Advisory Committee (LARMAC), it existed during the 1960s and '70s and offered L.A. musicians the opportunity to be a part of the pre-negotiation process.

Perhaps the most respected of the LARMAC team during that period was John Lowe, a studio saxophonist and member of the Local 47 board. According to composer-pianist Russ Freeman, a friend and fellow LARMAC member, Lowe was "a true spokesman, a true representative who always functioned in the best interests of musicians. He was looked up to by every musician I knew."

LARMAC members could advise Federation negotiators on proposed contract terms, "but we didn't have any actual authority," Freeman explained. "Occasionally we'd win a point or two, but most of the time we did not."

Throughout this era, the recording industry was bigger than ever. LPs were selling in the millions; blockbuster movies were demanding large orchestral scores; television, with its many variety shows, frequently featured big bands; and the jingle business was booming, particularly in New York and Chicago.

Recording musicians again began to feel that their contracts were not being properly negotiated. "The union didn't bother with us, because we were a small segment," New York percussionist Phil Kraus recalled. "Only about 200 or 300 fellows in New York were involved in recording."

Violinist Gene Orloff, a busy session player, felt that many elements of their contracts were unacceptable. "We would do recording dates of three hours, and we'd get a five-minute break. You'd

Phil Kraus, second RMA President 1971–1978

barely get [into the men's room] and zip down your pants when somebody was clapping to come on back," he said.

Also, he added, "we were not getting a nickel in residuals. We were having dates from 12 midnight to 3 in the morning, 11 at night to 2 in the morning, without any extra pay, working practically straight through. Conditions were intolerable. It was horrendous. We were musicians, but at the time we were treated like cattle."

Gene Orloff, first RMA President 1969–1971

Woodwind player Walt Levinsky noted: "The musicians felt we were getting absolutely zero help from the AF of M. I sat in as an observer on some of the negotiations and it was really silly. [Our representatives] would bluster, get up there and make a lot of speeches. It was a given that the networks would come out with exactly what they wanted – and what they were doing was chopping away at the business for years." Violinist Michael Comins recalled his embarrassment at the "bumbling" that took place in national contract negotiations during this period. "The players were being left out of the process," he said.

Orloff decided to organize a group of New York musicians who were active in the recording field, in hopes of pressuring the union to work harder on behalf of its members. He started with about 15 colleagues, mostly first-chair musicians (many of them also contractors) who, it was hoped, carried enough clout for union officials to pay attention.

They called themselves the Recording Musicians Association (RMA) and formally organized in 1969. Orloff was named first president, with fellow violinists Joe Malin and Julie Schachter as treasurer and secretary, respectively. Membership quickly mushroomed into the hundreds.

"At one point we called a meeting of the general membership, and an overwhelming number of musicians showed up," Orloff recalled. "I think it was close to 400, which was staggering at the time. [Usually] you'd call a [union] meeting and maybe 30, 40, 50 would show up. So when [union officials] saw that turnout, they understood that this was nothing to fool around with and that we were quite serious in our efforts."

Several of the early organizers credited Schachter with the lion's share of the work. Schachter, who had been concertmaster for Paul Whiteman, "deserves more credit than anybody involved in the RMA at that time," said Orloff. "When it came to do legwork and cajoling and threatening, Julie was the man who was always at everybody's disposal. He was a bulldog, personality-wise, and he wouldn't take no for an answer. He did 10 times as much for that organization as I did, or anyone else." Added Kraus: "Schachter was the brains behind the whole thing. He was kind of a financial wizard, too."

Kraus succeeded Orloff as president about 1971, and remained at the helm of the organization until he moved to Houston in 1978. Also in 1971, as a service to members, RMA began publishing membership directories and wage-scale booklets covering national contracts. These were largely the work of Malin, who remained RMA treasurer through 1984 and was probably best-known as Frank Sinatra's longtime contractor.

The strength of the new RMA enabled its officers to take part in jingle, video and phono contract negotiations. Jay Berliner, an active studio guitarist and later RMA International Secretary, joined the team in 1973. One of the busiest jingle players in the city, he kept meticulous personal records (on the advice of his father, an accountant) and soon became known as "Stats" for his thorough knowledge of session fees, residual payments and similar numbers.

"I was shocked by what I saw," Berliner remembered. "Al Knopf, vice president of Local 802, and Jack Fidel of the local's recording department, spoke on our behalf. Neither was able to follow what was going on. They would ask questions like, 'What's the rate for two to four men?' and 'When's lunch?'"

Tracking was a key issue in the 1973 jingle negotiations. Tracking (payment for previously recorded music being overdubbed by singers) had been given up in the 1969 phono agreement in return for a hefty increase in the scale rate. Berliner, based on an all-night search of his own records, attempted to explain that a similarly substantial session scale increase would be necessary to compensate for the loss of tracking money. "Henry Kaiser, the AFM general counsel and chief negotiator, wouldn't hear of it," Berliner later wrote. "There were no Federation or Local records to substantiate what I said."

Kaiser, arguably the nation's most famous labor lawyer, came up with a solution that cost jingle players a lot of money: the loss of tracking, a modest increase in the session scale, and a new dubbing formula that effectively combined into a 25 percent pay *cut*. The RMA launched a campaign to defeat the proposed agreement, but because the organization consisted solely of New York musicians, the AFM membership ratified it. Hundreds of musicians lost thousands of dollars as a result of the ignorance of the people who were being well-paid by the Federation to, ostensibly, look out for their interests.

"Henry Kaiser was an awesome figure," Berliner remarked. "A terrific orator, he really could expound on anything. He was a commanding presence. He'd enter a room immediately and you were

Jay Berliner, International RMA Secretary 1985-1995

aware of him; he had that flair for the dramatic. But he had two failings: he didn't know a thing about our business, and he was terrible in math." Added Comins: "In the forty-plus years since Kaiser negotiated some of our original contracts, we have never recovered from the losses, especially in the jingle business."

The RMA achieved its greatest success in those early years by reforming the pension fund.

Forced by the advent of the Musicians Guild to improve its benefits to members, the AFM in 1959 established an Employers Pension Welfare Fund (EPW, later EPF) in its contracts with the record business and the radio and TV networks. At first, only freelance musicians were eligible; in 1961, symphony players, arrangers, orchestrators and copyists were added to the list. The fund provides retirement benefits starting at age 55, plus death and disability benefits.

The idea was this: employers contribute a percentage directly to the fund based on the player's scale wages. It started out as little as 2 to 3 percent (and not all collective bargaining agreements included a pension provision), according to violist David Schwartz, who serves as the sole rank-and-file member of the fund's Board of Trustees and is vice president of the Los Angeles RMA. Today the standard contribution is 10 percent.

In the '70s, however, many musicians mistrusted the union and its handling of the mysterious pension fund. Schwartz recalled hearing people say, "Oh, you'll never see your money, it's down the drain."

RMA officials, too, were suspicious of the pension fund, particularly in view of the fact that officials routinely refused to divulge any details about their investments and the fund's overall worth. Legal counsel was retained in 1974 in an attempt to force the pension fund to open its books. (Top jingle writer-producer Steve Karmen recommended his own attorney, Allen Arrow, for

Dave Schwartz, AFM Pension Fund "rank and file" Trustee

the job, and offered to put up the money for legal fees until a fundraising campaign could be organized.)

That turned out to be unnecessary when Congress passed the Employee Retirement Income Security Act of 1974 (ERISA). ERISA provided for full disclosure of all pension-fund financial reports and investment information, and set certain standards in terms of operating funds in the best interests of their members.

With ERISA now the law of the land, Arrow succeeded in efforts to have RMA officers review the pension-fund books. They made detailed notes on investments and passed them along to Alvin Rogers, a studio drummer who was then studying for his stockbroker's license (and who later became a highly successful financial adviser).

Rogers told Jay Berliner that "it was the most pathetic portfolio he'd ever seen in his life" – part ownership of a bank in Schenectady, N.Y., a loan to a Catholic school in Staten Island, Pennsylvania Railroad bonds, mostly paying interest at a sorry 2 or 3 percent – all demonstrating "a total lack of financial expertise," said Berliner.

"The investment procedures were very suspect, and the fund wasn't growing terribly quickly," Comins confirmed. The money was apparently safe because so little money was being paid out, so it was a case of ineptness and not corruption, RMA officials decided.

Federation officers and pension fund trustees agreed to meet with Arrow and the RMA officers. "Out of this series of meetings came a plan calling for the total restructuring of the investment procedures of the pension fund," Berliner said. "A new system was created whereby the handling and selection of investments would be divided between two competing investment houses."

The airline pilots' association had been particularly successful in its investment strategy at the time, according to Kraus, and was used as a model.

Schwartz began looking into the pension fund in 1983. At that time, it had about $280 million in assets. Today it exceeds $1.1 billion. "That billion dollars is divided up between about a dozen different investment firms," he explained. About 60 percent of the fund is invested in stocks, about 35 percent in bonds, and only about 5 percent in the "government paper" that was once the primary investment of the fund.

As one of 14 trustees (seven from management, seven from the union) – and only the second rank-and-file musician ever to be chosen as a trustee, in 1995 – Schwartz interviews investment managers throughout the year. "Every three months they bring us a report on how they're doing," he said. "They are supposed to meet benchmarks in the stock market. If they don't meet these averages, they're put on notice and we can take away some of the money."

This investment-oversight strategy was a direct outgrowth of the RMA's insistence that the AFM pension fund be more responsible to the members. "The pension fund is so good today," said Schwartz, "that at the age of 60, a musician will get back all of the money he or she contributed to that fund in only two and a half years. So if that musician lives another 20 years, which is very likely today, he or she would collect eight times what they put in."

The RMA continued to gain in strength and influence within Local 802. As the '70s wore on, it participated in the formation of the Coordinated Musicians Committee to try and spur changes in the local; helped to write 802's Special Projects Fund bylaw; led the fight to upgrade 802's welfare plan and major medical benefits; and approved the use of Special Projects monies for a management consultant, modern cash registers and check files, microfilming of contracts, and increased check distribution personnel for 802's recording department.

With the active participation of RMA officers, national contract terms also improved. Observed Kraus: "We came in with the negotiating team from Local 802. And when they saw how adept we were at doing it, they didn't even show up at the negotiations. The only fellow who would come would be the vice president, Al Knopf."

Recording musicians were dealt a major blow, however, with the motion picture and television strike of 1980. At midnight on July 31, 5,000 Los Angeles musicians who were active in the film and TV scoring arena joined an estimated 60,000 actors from the Screen Actors Guild (SAG) and the American Federation of Television and Radio Artists (AFTRA), who were on strike against the Association of Motion Picture and Television Producers (AMPTP), which represented the major film and TV studios.

For the musicians, the issue was one of residuals for reruns of filmed television programs. Provisions for repayment to the musicians who had played on movie scores and in videotaped TV shows had been written into those contracts years ago, but had somehow been overlooked when the TV-film contract was first drawn up in the '50s. Actors, directors and writers had already achieved such benefits many years earlier.

Victor Fuentealba, AFM President Emeritus

"The musicians felt, and rightly so, that they should have the same benefits when their product is used again, whether it's videotape or television film," said Victor W. Fuentealba, who was then president of the Federation. "The emotions had built up through the years in this regard. That's what the players wanted."

Talks broke down over this issue. Unfortunately, a hoped-for solidarity between labor unions failed to materialize when SAG and AFTRA settled their strike after 11 weeks and actors began crossing musicians' picket lines. Even more shocking, the administration of Local 802 permitted union-sanctioned motion picture scoring dates. Max Arons, then president of 802, reportedly told members, "Play the dates. It's those jerks in L.A. who are on strike, not us!"

The AFM's strike against producers lasted 167 days. Musicians returned to work on January 15, 1981, having failed to win their key demand. "Ultimately, we settled a very bitter strike and got beat up pretty badly," reflected one prominent session player. "Once we went back to the table, there was severe retribution on the industry. We lost a great deal."

Most Hollywood musicians now feel that the strike was ill-advised. Fuentealba disagrees. "I feel that the strike was necessary," he said. "We had the support of the majority of our people at that time. In the long run, the musicians benefited, because there are times when that action has to be taken to demonstrate to management that you're not afraid to strike. This was one of the times when it was necessary. But we were dealing with a tough group of employers who probably realized that we couldn't win."

The anti-labor atmosphere made life more difficult for union workers in every realm of American life as Ronald Reagan (once president of the Screen Actors Guild) was elected to the Presidency in the fall of 1980. Reagan's failure to support unions in any sense – most publicly, when his actions cost hundreds of air-traffic controllers their jobs – cast a pall over the organized labor movement for the next eight years.

Michael Comins, who had become an active RMA member regularly attending contract negotiations, saw the need for a nationwide organization as early as 1977. He recalled a jingle negotiation where Los Angeles officials had done a better job with numbers than his Local 802 colleagues, and recommended "joining forces in some way" with similar contract proposals. "With one voice, we might get somewhere," he thought.

Chicago had, by this time, formed its own Association of Recording Musicians and was entertaining similar ideas. In an October 1979 letter to its New York counterpart, an advisory committee announced its "desire to form, post-haste, a national association of recording musicians [which] could aid the Federation in many ways including the negotiation of the several national contracts in which we, the recording musicians, are involved." It suggested American Association of Recording Musicians (AARM) as the name and recommended seeking conference status at AFM conventions.

In March 1981, the New York RMA made an even stronger proposal. "We need a national rank-and-file organization to deal with many of our problems," President Bernie Glow wrote the membership. "United in such a body, with a leadership role in the ratification process, we stand a better chance of getting much needed improvements in our profession." The proposed name: National Association of Recording Musicians (NARM).

By 1982, recording musicians around the country finally found a cause around which to unite. The rallying cry was an odd little phrase: Tuesday Productions.

THE TUESDAY DEAL SPURS A NATIONAL ALLIANCE

Tuesday Productions was a San Diego-based "jingle house": a company that specialized in creating music for television and radio commercials. It was a highly successful firm (with billings estimated in 1982 at $2 million per year), primarily because it was a non-union outfit. Tuesday offered cut-rate prices and the attractive – to some employers – prospect of not having to pay residuals to any performers.

The AFM objected to its practices, as did SAG and AFTRA (which represented singers). Tuesday filed unfair labor practice charges against the unions, and in 1979 sued AFTRA for antitrust violations including "secondary boycott" charges. A jury decided in Tuesday's favor, awarding more than $3 million in damages plus $1 million in legal fees, which because of the triple damages allowed under antitrust laws ended up totaling $10.5 million. The judgment forced AFTRA into bankruptcy in 1982.

Clearly concerned that AFM would be similarly targeted, AFM President Victor Fuentealba did not demand that Tuesday abide by the national jingles contract. Instead, in July 1982, he negotiated a separate agreement with Tuesday that called for a substantially lower scale rate ($40 per hour instead of $64.40), the elimination of residuals, and other elements that were far below AFM standards.

To Los Angeles musicians, especially those engaged in the jingle business, this was a "sweetheart deal" that threatened their livelihood. One of those musicians was a saxophone player and arranger named Dennis Dreith.

A Southern California native, Dreith had played road gigs for such top '60s groups as The Beach Boys and Paul Revere & The Raiders. In the studio, he had played on Phil Spector records and, in the '70s, began arranging for various performers including The O'Jays, Firefall and Stephen Bishop. By 1982, he was part of a music house that was actively pursuing jingle work. Dreith was writing horn and rhythm charts for national spots like Taco Bell and

Dennis Dreith, RMA President 1986-

International House of Pancakes, and regional ones for such clients as Pacific Southwest Airlines.

"We were one of the music houses that had been playing by the rules," Dreith recalled, "and the [Tuesday] guys who had been the scab outfit, undercutting all this, now had a union contract. Any advertising agency could go to them for their regional spots – it was much cheaper. So it was just devastating. Overnight, it cost us huge amounts of money."

Dreith met with one of his competitors, fellow L.A. jingle packager John Andrew Tartaglia, and together they telephoned Fuentealba directly in hopes of discussing the now-controversial pact. According to Dreith, the union president treated them rudely, claiming it was none of their business and refusing to discuss the Tuesday terms.

For Dreith, it was a startling awakening and – although he didn't yet realize it – the beginning of a second career as a union activist. Dreith and Tartaglia contacted many of the other L.A. jingle producers and called a meeting at Local 47 headquarters. Dreith, who had never before addressed a public gathering, quietly read a simple statement expressing his feelings. To his surprise, the crowd of 200 fellow musicians cheered wildly.

Recording musicians in New York and Chicago (two cities with even more jingle business than Los Angeles) were equally outraged about the Tuesday agreement. As veteran jingle player Jay Berliner later wrote, "Tuesday's so-called 'local' music tracks were being used on jingles, promos and IDs airing all over the United States and posed a serious threat to the work being done under the AFM national agreements."

New York's RMA joined forces with the Society of Advertising Music Producers, Arrangers and Composers, Inc. (SAMPAC) to demand that the AFM rescind the Tuesday contract. In a joint statement issued in October 1982, they referred to the contract terms as "the most massive giveback in the history of labor relations." They pointed out that "it will be impossible to compete with a producer who can legally offer music in every market at a greatly reduced rate with no residuals... The contract represents nothing more than legitimizing non-union conditions that have existed for years, while throwing away a quarter-century of progress that has been achieved through years of arduous negotiation."

Daily Variety referred to the reaction in the affected locals as "bitter and frequently vitriolic." The administrations of locals 47, 802, 10-208 (Chicago) and 257 (Nashville) forced a special meeting of the Federation's International Executive Board (IEB) in early November. The IEB voted to instruct Fuentealba and his negotiating subcommittee to meet with Tuesday in an attempt to "mutually rescind" the contract.

Fuentealba was opposed to such a move but agreed to abide by the wishes of the IEB. Tuesday, having cut the greatest deal in the history of commercial music, wasn't about to give it up, and the contract remained in force for the next two years. In fact, despite vocal opposition by recording musicians – and demonstrable proof that it was costing legitimate, union-affiliated producers business – Fuentealba renewed the agreement in June 1984 (this time for three years, although it was actually terminated in March 1986).

Fuentealba maintained throughout, and has since, that the Tuesday deal was designed to "legitimize in some fashion" their policies while trying to protect the rest of the industry. "I don't think that the agreement that was eventually signed adversely affected our negotiations with the industry," he insisted, "and although it was naturally raised by them at certain points in the negotiations, we were able to restrict it in such a fashion that it did not impact on the national agreement. What we did was the best that could be done under the circumstances. I don't think there was a choice."

The Tuesday Deal

Walt Levinsky, first International RMA President 1983-1986

The result of the Tuesday Productions controversy was a mobilization of American and Canadian recording musicians in a way that had not previously been possible. "Tuesday was the rallying cry," said Berliner. "That really helped us organize."

Walt Levinsky had been elected president of New York's Recording Musicians Association in May 1981. His precedessor, trumpeter Bernie Glow, had asked the composer/arranger/woodwind player and savvy New Jersey politician to take over the RMA (Glow had been diagnosed with cancer). Levinsky felt that he couldn't refuse after being given a standing ovation by the membership upon being introduced as the "nominee."

Before long, Levinsky realized that the solely New York-based RMA needed the help of their fellow musicians in other key cities. "We weren't going to accomplish anything unless we had an international, or at least a national, RMA," he said. "We had no strength. We were totally without leverage. We were a crowd of about 300 members, but most of them were inactive. We used to get 30 or 40 people to an RMA meeting."

Michael Comins, first International RMA Secretary 1983-1985

Levinsky and vice president Michael Comins decided to fly to Chicago, Nashville, Los Angeles and Toronto – the other four primary recording centers in North America – to try and convince studio players to join a larger, more powerful organization. They visited Chicago and L.A. on the weekend of December 5-6, 1982, Toronto on Feb. 13, 1983, and Nashville on March 12.

"We found enthusiasm everywhere," Levinsky said. "In every town, people were trying to preserve what they had. Even if we didn't make any gains, we didn't want to keep having losses. All the top studio guys were at the meetings. Marvelous players." Levinsky, a seasoned public speaker, was convincing. He pointed out the need for political clout within the Federation. "It was just the right time to consolidate and try and use our leverage," he said.

"Walt was the consummate politician," Comins said. "Without him, I don't know how successful we would have been. He was great at smoothing out the rough edges. I was the guy who got up and yelled and screamed, damning the Federation and the contract process."

The Tuesday deal wasn't the only issue on the table. The growing influence of synthesizers as a possible replacement for live musicians was also of grave concern. Comins had assembled a tape of a Synclavier playing five different combinations of "orchestral" music. "I saw harp players turn white when they heard the harp sound," Comins recalled. "And French horn players, and so forth."

Contractor/flutist Joe Soldo (who had been a member of the New York RMA prior to his move to Los Angeles in 1971, and whose ex-partner Joe Malin was treasurer in New York) and violinist Sheldon Sanov organized the Los Angeles chapter in early January 1983. Sanov volunteered to serve as the first president, Soldo as treasurer. At first, only about 60 or 70 musicians of the approximately 400 full-time studio players in Local 47 signed up. "A lot of players were afraid because of the Guild," Sanov noted. "A lot of people got burned [by that experience]."

Nonetheless, the Tuesday deal galvanized many of the musicians. "Our fear, and it turned out to be true," Sanov added, "was that management would bring this up at the [upcoming jingle] negotiations. And sure enough, they did. It was on the table. So it was critical that we were there, as an effective counter-force to represent our players right from the beginning, along with New York and Chicago."

By the jingle negotiations of April 1983, the Los Angeles Recording Musicians Advisory Committee (LARMAC), created in 1961 to consult with Federation officials on collective bargaining matters, had been dormant for years.

But Dick Gabriel, who had worked for Cecil Read in the national contracts division at Local 47 in the late '70s and who opened the Federation's West Coast recording office in 1980, called Dreith after hearing him speak on the Tuesday Productions issue. Gabriel suggested resurrecting LARMAC and Dreith was named its chairman. Shortly thereafter, Dreith also joined the RMA.

The International RMA was still in its formative stages; the first meeting of its newly constituted international board wouldn't be held for several more months. But with chapters now being launched in four more cities and the national jingle negotiation soon to be held, the leaders of the RMA came up with a plan that would ensure that its voice would be heard.

Historically, each of the major locals came in to the first pre-negotiation caucus with its own proposals for contract terms. In fact, recalled Dreith, "up to this time, there had been a great deal of animosity and suspicion between musicians in Los Angeles and New York. The purpose of the RMA – more than saving the jingle contract – was to create unity among recording musicians in every part of the United States and Canada. We're doing basically the same work. What's the difference between playing in a recording studio in New York, Los Angeles, Nashville, Chicago or Toronto?"

So with this goal in mind, RMA set out to coordinate, in advance, all five jingle-contract proposals. With New York's Berliner as the statistics maven and Los Angeles' Dreith as researcher and reviewer of contract language, the five proposals were examined, evaluated and assimilated into a single unified contract proposal.

According to Comins, five identical proposals – each labeled with the newly designed RMA logo – were presented at that first caucus. Fuentealba and his negotiating subcommittee had no choice but to present to management the initiatives that the RMA had assembled and been individually endorsed by the locals in each of the five major recording cities.

(One of the RMA's key demands was the principle of "session and use," which SAG and AFTRA singers had won years earlier: one payment for the session, a second payment for actual use on the air. AFM contract language had always included use during the first 13-week cycle as part of the session fee, which covered the recording of three spots. Fuentealba fought hard for the concept during the 1983 negotiations, according to several observers, but it wasn't actually won until 1991.)

"That first jingle negotiation was very, very stormy," Dreith recalled. "It was unbelievably intense. Between Fuentealba and myself, there was a great deal of mistrust." Complicating matters was the fact that the LARMAC/RMA team was only allowed into negotiations as observers. They could make no statements. "We were allowed comments at caucus," Dreith explained, "but even that was acrimonious."

Many Federation officials regarded the newly unified, multi-city RMA with distrust, even paranoia. Sanov recalled, "We went through World War III to make sure we were represented there." Levinsky: "They were fearful. They didn't want another Guild situation." Dreith: "The first thing the Federation thought was: The

International RMA forms: Joe Soldo, Walt Levinsky, Sheldon Sanov and Dennis Dreith

Guild is back. The phrase 'dual unionism' was bantered around many times."

On June 27, 1983, the Recording Musicians of America formally filed its certificate of incorporation. Levinsky was president, Sanov vice president, Comins secretary and Soldo treasurer. (The name was later altered to Recording Musicians Association of the United States and Canada, maintaining the acronym RMA. It has since become better known as the International RMA.)

"This was a most important time in RMA history," Dreith reflected. "It totally revamped the whole situation with the locals. It put us in the midst of things. From that point forward, RMA has been firmly established as a part of the negotiating process."

It continued – but didn't get any easier – through the contract negotiations of 1983 and 1984 in all other areas: videotape, phonograph, motion picture, TV film. Dreith became more and more active with the organization, joining its board and accompanying Levinsky on visits to many of the AFM conferences around the country. On board during negotiations was well-liked RMA attorney Ned Parsekian, a former New Jersey state senator and one-time head of the New Jersey Crime Commission. "Ned talked of issues of courage and ethics," Dreith said, "and in many ways, set a standard in terms of establishing ethical guidelines for ourselves."

The first meeting of the International board of directors was held in September 1983 in Nashville. Federation counsel Cos Abato attended the meeting and, again raising the spectre of "dual unionism," challenged its authority; Parsekian later wrote an opinion refuting this claim.

Only months after its formation, the International RMA already boasted more than 1,000 members. Now that it represented the majority of recording musicians in North America, Levinsky wanted a much higher degree of recognition for the RMA. "We should

Eddy Arnold Show, Nashville (CBS 1949)
(L-R) Skeeter Willis, Vic Willis, Owen Bradley, Roy Wiggins,
Eddy Arnold, Chuck Wright, Harold Bradley

have a seat at the convention," he believed. Levinsky and Dreith (designated a "presidential assistant") attended the 1985 AFM convention in Charleston, W. Va. Their treatment was indicative of how Federation officials perceived the RMA.

"Our goal was to come away with conference status," Levinsky recalled. "When we got there, we were really sloughed off." They were not even seated on the convention floor; instead, they were relegated to the back-of-the-hall "peanut gallery," where wives, guests and observers were seated. "It was unconscionable. I was so angry. I lit into the president of the Toronto local," Levinsky said. It worked. The next day, they were invited to sit on the dais and were formally introduced as the representatives of the RMA.

Conference status was already conferred on the International Conference of Symphony and Opera Musicians (ICSOM), formed in 1962; the Organization of Canadian Symphony Musicians (OCSM), formed in 1974; and the Regional Orchestra Players Association (ROPA), formed in 1984. According to Dreith, it was a showy title that had little meaning in terms of power within the Federation. But once conference status was achieved, the idea went, perhaps that power could be discovered and developed.

Dreith, who had succeeded Sanov as president of the Los Angeles chapter, became, in June 1986, Levinsky's hand-picked successor as president of the International RMA as well. "I thought he was the brightest, the least controversial. He had a real fervor for this." For Levinsky, who "was never all that interested in union politics" anyway, it was time to step down. He was especially disappointed to discover that many top musicians, including some of those closest to him, had been playing non-union dates during the time he was trying to raise the consciousness of all recording musicians within the AFM.

Levinsky was named president emeritus. "I think I did give the musicians some sense of hope," he later reflected. "I was trying to get [the RMA] strong enough to where we had some real leverage and we could go in and insist on certain things with the Federation."

The growing political clout of the RMA became apparent in early 1987. During the "phono" (record) negotiations that began in November 1986, the major record companies again made clear that their primary goal was the elimination of the Music Performance Trust Fund and the decimation of the Special Payments Fund.

The Music Performance Trust Fund (MPTF) was created in 1948 by then-AFM President James C. Petrillo to provide free live-music concerts around the country, in part because the newly popular recording medium of phonograph records was (theoretically) depriving musicians of work. A tiny percentage of the sale of records and tapes has been paid by the record companies ever since, providing an estimated 35,000 performances of live music every year in venues that include parks, libraries, churches, hospitals, senior citizen homes and mental health facilities.

There are two Special Payments Funds (SPF). One, which relates to record albums, was the result of the 1961 Guild-dissolution agreement that allowed musicians to collect half the MPTF royalty on records to which they contribute; it first took effect in 1964. The other, which relates to movies, allows musicians who performed on specific film scores to collect a small percentage of the profits made when those films are sold to secondary markets (TV, home video, etc.); it started in 1972.

As the years went by, the record industry balked at making these payments, contending that the music-in-the-park notion of the MPTF was passé and that the SPF was excessive considering the money already being paid to session players.

In 1983, for example, manufacturers were determined to decimate both funds. Industry was represented by Norman Samnick, then a vice president at Warner Bros., and as described by Berliner, "a man of considerable wit and of very considerable girth; he weighed well over 300 pounds." Berliner recounted the events of Nov. 30, 1983: "Vic Fuentealba was determined to stand his ground. On the last day of the agreement, Vic, in perhaps his finest hour, had the building maintenance staff cut off all air conditioning to the AFM offices. We went into a marathon, non-stop negotiation, allowing no food or drink to be brought in. He was determined to starve Samnick into submission. (Vic, in preparation for this, had loaded up his office with fruit, cold beverages, etc. He was wearing his most comfortable and light shirt.) By 5:30 that afternoon, the negotiations were over. The funds were saved."

In spite of Fuentealba's efforts, however, the industry had succeeded in making significant cuts to the contributions formula of the MPTF. Federation auditors claimed that those cuts resulted in negligible reductions in contributions, although RMA officials later charged that "significant bookkeeping changes in the MPTF's annual reports... were designed to conceal the severity of the damage that had been inflicted on the MPTF."

It was now January 1987. "Our goal was to have absolutely no cuts to the funds," Dreith stated. He, and a strong contingent of RMA representatives and leaders from six locals, were at the negotiations in New York. "We were drafting the proposals [although] our official status was that of observer," Dreith continued. "Victor [Fuentealba] was an attorney; he wanted to negotiate. We weren't happy with the way he was negotiating."

Fuentealba's dilemma: how hard a line to take with the record companies and, if there was no room for compromise, should he authorize a strike over the funds? "It was a difficult negotiation and we weren't making much progress," he recalled. "It was always my philosophy that if you're going to strike, you'd better have your troops behind you, because once you make that step, you can't

Nashville studio musicians at a 1960's New York record date for Mercury Records; (L-R) top: Pique Robbins, Bob Moore, Harold Bradley, Boots Randolph, Kelso Herston; middle: Ray Stevens, Jerry Kennedy; bottom: Bill Justis, Charlie McCoy

turn around and capitulate. Unless we were united, a strike would be a mistake."

Nashville's player representatives had informed Fuentealba that they would not support a strike. On the other hand, Local 47 President Bernie Fleischer had presented a petition signed by the entire Los Angeles Philharmonic that no changes to the funds would be acceptable under any circumstances. Instead of accepting the no-cuts position of the RMA, Fuentealba decided to negotiate with the record companies in hopes of finding an acceptable compromise and submitting it to the membership for a vote.

When talk of a plateau – MPTF and SPF payments kicking in only after 25,000 units are sold – became AFM strategy, Dreith drew the line. Fuentealba pointed out that a strike could mean the end of the funds, and he suggested that Dreith and Fleischer did not, in fact, represent the majority of the affected musicians. Fuentealba wanted to negotiate a deal and take it back to the membership (with the ballot to be marked "ratify" or "strike").

It was the most intense moment in the history of the RMA, and one that bore a striking sense of déjà vu for both the Federation and recording musicians: MPTF payments had been a crucial factor in the formation of the Guild 30 years earlier. The AFM president insisted that he was right; the RMA president knew that he could not go along with this. According to an observer at the session, after Toronto local president Bobby Herriot called the Federation president "nothing but a dictator" and stomped out, Fuentealba turned to the group and said, "Who are you to tell me what to do?"

Dreith, speaking in angry but measured tones, told Fuentelaba: "It's apparent that you don't care about what we have to say. You are allowing us no input in this negotiation. Our presence here is superfluous. We won't walk down this road with you. It's your contract, Victor. It's your negotiation. We'll have nothing to do with it." He, and all of the union officials and RMA representatives from all five locals, got up and walked out.

The action was unprecedented. Dreith – who actually had decertification papers in his briefcase, should things go completely and irrevocably wrong with the AFM – said he didn't want to break away as the Guild had. "I've always taken the dimmest view of decertification of any of our officers. It's something that you do not want to do." But AFM officials weren't sure what was happening. To some, the spectre of the Guild was back. "It was a very awkward situation to be in," Fuentealba later acknowledged.

A representative from the Nashville local later returned to the talks. By the end of the day, the two sides had reached a tentative agreement that included, in Fuentealba's words, "cuts which we felt would not decimate the funds." The leaders of the New York, Los Angeles and Chicago locals campaigned against the agreement, estimating that the 25,000-unit sales plateau could mean a cut in fund contributions from 10 to 40 percent. Federation members ratified it anyway, 1,153-844. (And, as it turned out, research later indicated that the effects of the new plateau were negligible.)

When he took office in 1978, Fuentealba was "a breath of fresh air," Berliner said. "Here was an intelligent guy who listened. He had a pretty good picture of what the business was like. Also, he was an excellent administrator. The morale among the employees at the Federation had never been so good. Victor's failing was that he sometimes did things on his own that drove us crazy. He didn't trust people; he didn't realize who his friends were."

Now, as a result of the breakdown over the phono negotiations, Fuentealba lost his allies at the major locals and it would cost him his presidency.

As the June 1987 AFM convention approached, leaders of the New York, Los Angeles and Chicago locals, feeling their recommendations – and thus, their constituencies – had been unjustly ig-

(L-R): Sheridon Stokes, Sheldon Sanov, Dennis Dreith, Marty Emerson (AFM President), Dick Gabriel (Assistant to the President, AFM Recording Department), Ray Kelley, Catherine Gotthoffer, Joe Brooks, David Schwartz

nored, began to push for "increased democratization" within the Federation. More to the point, they called for a draft of Secretary-Treasurer Emeritus J. Martin "Marty" Emerson as president.

In the meantime, Los Angeles RMA member Ray Kelley had created a new organization, Americans for Live Music, which was specifically designed to call attention to and ultimately save the MPTF. "We did a huge mailing," said cellist Tony Cooke, who helped coordinate the effort. "Every record company, every receiver of the funds, every place we could think of, and it created an amazing outpouring of support for preserving the trust fund."

Individual RMA members financially supported the Emerson candidacy and, for the first time, the RMA hosted a hospitality suite at the Las Vegas hotel hosting the convention. Fuentealba's opening address, which took the RMA and the major-local presidents to task for the events of earlier in the year (labeling the walkout "immature" and "damaging to our bargaining posture"), stirred emotions even more. The next day, Fleischer delivered a scathing rebuttal that accused the president of "awful departures from the truth."

Emerson won the election, 708-650. It was the first time in the history of the AFM that a sitting president had been ousted. Fuentealba didn't go down without a fight, however. In July, he filed a formal challenge, asking the International Executive Board to set aside the Emerson victory because of alleged violations of the Landrum-Griffin Act (specifically "improper use of official publications, letterheads and union funds").

A federal district court ruled the election invalid and ordered a new election, this time to be supervised by the Department of Labor. Instead of holding a special election, however, it occurred at the 1989 convention – tightly controlled by Labor Department regulations and officials, which irritated delegates – and Emerson was reaffirmed as president.

Further fallout directly affected the RMA. The Department of Labor investigation into the Fuentealba election included a probe of RMA activities and literature, because much of what RMA published in recent months had been critical of the AFM president.

"The letters we wrote criticizing Victor were about issues, not about the election, so we were totally clean," Dreith noted. But the Department of Labor, in examining the structure and activities of RMA, made a ruling that it is a labor organization subject to all of the constraints and obligations of a local union.

"It made us operate a little more tightly," said Dreith. "It gave us credibility in Washington, and made us function in a more professional way. At the time it was a real nuisance, but in retrospect it was actually a very good thing." RMA has weathered several DOL investigations since that time, "some extensive, some very minor," Dreith added.

FOR THE RECORD

CONFERENCE STATUS, CONFLICT IN L.A., AND GROWTH INTERNATIONALLY

With the 1987 convention, the RMA had come of age and into its own. Former RMA officers who were delegates to the convention were able to offer resolutions in support of RMA ideals. Two of those were important not only to the RMA but to members throughout the Federation.

The first was an expansion of the nature of "conference status." Prior to 1987, only geographical areas (the regional conferences such as Western, New York State, etc.) and symphony musicians (the player conferences ICSOM, ROPA and OCSM) were able to petition for conference status. A resolution at the convention broadened the definition so that any group of players could apply; the IEB formally granted RMA conference status at its September 1987 meeting.

Conference status was, at first, merely "window dressing," Dreith explained. Having been granted that standing, the RMA began working behind the scenes – dealing with Federation officers and delegates, visiting other conferences – to beef up the definition.

That happened at the 1989 AFM convention. "Now," Dreith pointed out, "conference status gives us the right to propose legislation at the convention; to speak on any legislation, not just what we propose; and the right to appear before various committees of the convention. We don't have a vote; but much better than a vote, we have a voice at the convention." Also part of conference status: institutional access to the IEB and the subcommittees.

"We're an inside part of the team," Dreith said. "It has the least glamor, but in essence it changed the face of the AFM, probably forever. Our conference status started a whole chain of events. It made [the AFM] a true democratic union."

Equally important to members of the Federation, ratification language was added to the by-laws for the first time. While this had long been a policy of the AFM (dating back to the agreement to dissolve the Guild), it had never been formalized. Now, any collective bargaining agreement would have to be submitted to a secret-ballot ratification vote of eligible members.

As the RMA became a rising power within the AFM, however, it found itself battling the leadership of the local that boasted the largest RMA membership: Local 47 in Los Angeles.

Flutist Bernie Fleischer was elected president of Local 47 at the end of 1984. Run-ins with Sanov and Dreith, then the leaders of the Los Angeles RMA chapter, began during the fall campaign (when Fleischer accused them of breaking a promise to stay neutral, something they denied). Tensions escalated and "constant battles" with Fleischer occurred throughout his first three years in office, Dreith said. (Fleischer declined to be interviewed for this chronicle.)

Several observers quoted Fleischer as saying that he would "destroy the RMA." In late 1988, AFM President Marty Emerson announced that Dreith – now president of the International RMA – would become the first player representative ever to sit on the AFM's negotiating subcommittee. (Ironically, Dreith's work commitments precluded him from actually serving; Jay Berliner took his place.)

The appointment was hailed by recording musicians as a big step forward for the rank-and-file. It was, however, opposed by Fleischer and ignited a heated conflict with the Los Angeles RMA chapter that would take considerable time, energy and money for the next two years. In February, Fleischer ignored a 200-signature petition to have Local 47 sponsor an RMA representative to the upcoming jingle negotiations.

The April RMA newsletter stated that this marked "the first time in 13 consecutive negotiations that a [Los Angeles] representative active in the industry has been denied sponsorship." In addition, it referred to "other non-cooperative actions by Fleischer undermining effective representation of recording musicians [that] give us cause for serious concern."

Response was immediate. The May edition of Local 47's *Overture* newsletter carried a Fleischer column critical of the RMA-requested audit of the Motion Picture Special Payments Fund. Even more critical was a letter from Local 47 Trustee Chase Craig attacking the Los Angeles RMA in no uncertain terms.

Craig referred to its "irrational, non-thinking, elitist hierarchy," accused them of creating "an unsigned politically oriented poison-pen letter" and declared the L.A. chapter "a disgrace as an organization." Dreith responded to both in the next issue, attempting to set the record straight about Fleischer's charges (the audit would not be paid by local musicians) and Craig's (outlining the RMA's position at the jingle negotiations which was the springboard for the letter).

"The letter was meant to incite," Craig later explained. "There was a certain amount of apathy within the RMA at that time. They were definitely not turning out to meetings; they were more or less giving Dennis complete carte blanche. There was distrust even at the Federation level: 'Dennis is here making his case, but does it really reflect these people? Is this just a very small group leading a herd?' These were questions being asked.

Chase Craig, Director AFM Electronic Music Services Division (EMSD)

"They had to come out and show their strength. What better way to get them to come out than to call them a bunch of names and tell them that Dennis is going off half-cocked?"

As a tactic, it could hardly have been more successful. Nearly 700 people showed up at a special July meeting (including virtually all of the 500 RMA members in Local 47). Craig remembered it as "a very contentious meeting," but one where he took the microphone to acknowledge that his assertions in the May letter – notably that the RMA was not reflecting the desires of its members – were clearly wrong.

"If I personally had any doubts, there was no question at the end of that meeting," Craig said. Fleischer, however, was "absolutely furious," he noted, "shouting and yelling at people... He could see nothing but black. That was where Bernie and I parted completely."

Strong turnout by RMA members at subsequent Local 47 meetings forced the dismissal of Bleiweiss Communications, a public-relations firm which RMA officials claimed was being used to malign the organization in print; and led recording musicians to vote for a reduction in National Contract work dues. Fleischer viewed both actions as hurtful to the membership of the local.

By November, the skirmishes had escalated into full-scale war. Fleischer sent out a detailed, four-page "report to the membership" headlined "Do You Know That Your Union Is Being Stolen?" and subtitled "The History of a Power Play." In it, he charged that "the RMA has undertaken an unrelenting campaign of distortion, falsehoods and personal attacks on me and my wife, Local 47 staff member Dee Dee Daniel." And, he stated that "Musicians' Local 47 is a frighteningly short time away from being taken over by a small activist, albeit tyrannical, substantially unqualified, minority of recording musicians."

The RMA, which at the time was backing an amendment to the by-laws allowing a recall of officers, responded two weeks later: "We are attempting to save our union from financial ruin brought about by the worst case of fiscal mismanagement by any administration in the history of Local 47." The RMA brochure portrayed Fleischer as "confused and irrational. His complete disregard of the truth has allowed him to make outrageous and distorted state-

FOR THE RECORD

Brian O'Connor, RMA Executive Board 1995-

ments." The recall provision managed a 55 percent plurality but failed to muster the necessary two-thirds vote in order to pass.

Fleischer asked the International Executive Board to investigate RMA, accusing it of "obstructing the local's affairs," but the IEB dismissed the charges as "without merit."

At the same time, Local 47 became embroiled in litigation on several fronts. A lawsuit was filed against Walt Disney Productions in an attempt to recover millions allegedly owed on 1948-60 music (which the RMA contended was a misreading of contractual obligations and attempted to derail before the upcoming film negotiations); French horn player Brian O'Connor, later an RMA board member, filed federal charges against Fleischer for violating his First Amendment rights; and several other cases were pending.

The O'Connor case was an unfortunate example. A highly regarded horn player, O'Connor was one of several musicians who wrote Fleischer asking for help in solving a complex problem involving union and non-union musicians at a Pasadena theater company in early 1987; 34 other affected musicians also signed the letter. Fleischer's response was to single out O'Connor and file charges against him, which the Local 47 trial board dismissed. O'Connor asked for reimbursement of his $5,000-plus legal fees. Hearing nothing in response, O'Connor filed suit in Federal District Court, charging that Fleischer had violated his freedom-of-speech rights. A four-year court case ensued, and after Fleischer was ousted from office, Local 47 lawyers advised immediate settlement because O'Connor's case was so strong. "If Bernie had talked to us in the first place," O'Connor later said, "it wouldn't have cost a cent."

"Bernie made some serious mistakes. He alienated certain members," recalled Max Herman, who came out of retirement to head a slate that defeated Fleischer in the December 1990 election. The O'Connor case alone cost the local more than $110,000, Herman said. The Disney suit was "frivolous," he added, and seriously damaged

FOR THE RECORD

Fleischer's Actions Cost Local 47 More Than $110,000

Overture

PUBLISHED MONTHLY BY LOCAL 47, LOS ANGELES, AMERICAN FEDERATION OF MUSICIANS (AFL-CIO)

VOLUME 71 MAY 1991 NO. 1

O'CONNOR'S FIGHT FOR MEMBERS' RIGHT TO FREEDOM OF SPEECH!

Local 47 Settles Free Speech Lawsuit with O'Connor

One of our longtime members — who in 1987 originally sued former President Bernie Fleischer for punitive damages — has settled with Local 47 for an apology, legal fees, one dollar in punitive damages and only minimum compensation for lost time from work.

Brian O'Connor, a french horn player who was singled out by former President Bernie Fleischer and charged with committing "a breach of good faith", is now being hailed as a union hero by the new administration for:

— standing up for freedom of speech for all union members.

— making a courageous stand that appears to have saved Local 47 from completing a substandard agreement.

— saving the union an untold amount of money by agreeing to a settlement substantially less than that which Local 47 believed recoverable at trial. O'Connor agreed to a settlement that pays legal fees, $2,000 for lost income due to testimony and appearances, and a printed letter of apology.

What began as a letter of concern by 35 members escalated into formal charges against O'Connor only, and into a legal battle that threatened to ruin the local. The entire story follows, starting on page 12.

PRESIDENT'S MESSAGE

The Lawsuit Is Finally Over

As this issue points out, a damaging lawsuit has been settled. It has been settled because calm and responsible people prevailed and I would like to publicly thank those who made this reasonable conclusion possible.

First of all I would like to thank Brian O'Connor. It was clear from the moment the new administration took office that he was more interested in the welfare of the union than in receiving punitive damages. Then I would like to thank and pay tribute to the Executive Board who acted in a reasonable and professional manner. I would also like to thank the attorneys, Howard S. Vallens, of Buckner & Haile, who represented Mr. O'Connor, was clearly interested in upholding freedom of speech and properly representing his client, and conducted himself in a manner that brings credit to the legal profession. Abe Levy, who represents Local 47, did everything possible to bring this case to a speedy conclusion.

Finally I would like to thank Shed Behar, who followed a simple directive to "make things right" and did an outstanding job of investigating the matter and writing an objective and responsible account of the events.

Max Herman

This story has been prepared by Local 47 from court records and sworn testimony as part of the settlement of a lawsuit with Brian O'Connor. The Local 47 Board of Directors has agreed to publish a letter of apology in Overture, as well as publish a complete chronology of events and all pertinent documents.

The story is an attempt by the present administration to outline the events in a sequence that will be understandable to our readers. The praise for Mr. O'Connor has not been requested by him or his attorneys. It is a unanimous acknowledgement by the Board of Directors of a courageous man, who stood up for fairness, decency and the rights of all Local 47 members to freely express themselves.

LETTER OF APOLOGY TO BRIAN O'CONNOR
SEE PAGE 12

the AFM in the eyes of Disney management. "Bernie's a talented guy, but [being president] went to his head a little bit," Herman said.

The 1990 election campaign was, by all accounts, brutal and negative in the extreme. RMA members solicited campaign contributions under the banner Musicians for a New Administration (with an MNA logo very similar to that of the RMA) and urged election of the Herman slate, more than half of which consisted of members previously aligned with Fleischer.

The anti-Fleischer campaign, however, made a colossal blunder. In a vicious, eight-page diatribe mailed to the Local 47 membership, a coalition of musicians calling itself the Committee to Restore Integrity accused Fleischer of ordering Local 47's Health Fund manager to "commit a felony" by falsifying records. Fleischer sued several officers of the RMA, and the organization itself, for slander and libel. The RMA was dropped from the case in May 1992, but the other defendants eventually settled out of court.

With Herman – an RMA supporter, having been a studio musician in the '40s and '50s – back at the helm, the atmosphere at Local 47 was again friendly to recording musicians. Herman settled all the lawsuits, apologized to Disney executives (who had begun to go overseas to record their theme-park music) and attempted to move ahead with union business.

In the meantime, with its newly empowered conference status in place, RMA was making strides within the AFM and the recording industry as a whole. In March 1990, RMA representatives were instrumental in adding a "joint cooperative committee" provision to the film and television agreement negotiated with the Alliance of Motion Picture and Television Producers (AMPTP).

The purpose of this committee was, and is, "to address and endeavor to resolve any item of mutual concern on an industry-wide or individual-producer basis... in lieu of grievance and arbitration"

– in other words, for producers and musicians to talk with each other to try and resolve problems that may arise between contract negotiations. Joint Cooperative Committees were eventually added to all AFM agreements.

In some cases, these units existed in contract language but were never activated, Dreith explained. "It's the most dramatic thing to happen in collective bargaining in all the time I've been involved in negotiations. This is the future of labor-management relations. It gives us a chance, outside of the pressure-cooker of negotiations, to sit down in a non-confrontational way and work out our differences. In every case, we come away understanding each others' problems much better."

One of the most innovative solutions to emerge from the film/TV joint cooperative committee was the so-called low-budget film agreement, reached in March 1994. That enables films under $12 million (and many TV-movies and miniseries) to be eligible for a break of about one-third in the cost of musicians, as well as a reduction in the soundtrack-album rate for repayment of musicians.

The low-budget agreement was, in part, a response to the continuing problem of producers going elsewhere to record music for films and TV. The issue dates back to the 1980s, when Fleischer formally complained to the United States Olympic Committee about the London scoring of *16 Days of Glory*, the official film of the 1984 Olympics in Los Angeles.

It reached a crisis stage in the early '90s, when composers began regularly recording film and TV scores in Salt Lake City, Utah. The ability to record on a non-union basis (lower scales, no overtime, no doubles, no pension payments, no re-use payments, etc.) enabled producers to save as much as 50 percent on their music budgets. The issue was so hot that then-AFM President Mark Tully Massagli (elected in 1991) visited Los Angeles in February 1992 and addressed the concerns of the L.A. musicians about the vast amount of work that was leaving town. (By 1996, London and Seattle had replaced Salt Lake as the non-AFM venues of choice for producers looking to trim costs.)

New chapters of RMA began to spring up. While the Toronto and Chicago chapters disappeared, recording musicians in Spokane,

Richard Totusek (L), RMA International Vice President, 1990- with Tony Cooke, RMA International Treasurer

Wash., Orlando, Fla., and Northern California (based in San Jose) joined under the RMA banner.

Pianist Richard Totusek, longtime union activist who was president of the Spokane local and served on the International Executive Board, became such a strong ally of the RMA that he moved to Los Angeles in 1993 and was elected vice president, and later treasurer, of Local 47.

Totusek heard such negative things about the RMA from then-AFM President Victor Fuentealba that, when he later met Walt Levinsky and his colleagues, he said "I was quite amazed because I couldn't find either the horns or the tails that I had been told to expect."

Rather, he said, "these were some of the most intelligent and perceptive people that I had ever met. It was not true that they were super-reactionaries determined not to allow any change. Actually, they perceived that there was a need for change but that it had to be done without harming what they had and what they were doing."

In fact, it was Totusek, during his time in Spokane and on the IEB, who championed the limited-pressing agreement approved by the Federation in 1987. That allows records and tapes intended for limited distribution to be recorded under union auspices but at more affordable rates. Totusek also drafted the legislation enabling the RMA to achieve conference status; completely recodified the Federation by-laws; and, because of his encyclopedic knowledge of Robert's Rules of Order, served as parliamentarian for all of the symphonic conferences for many years.

Totusek also chaired the AFM's Trade Division study committee, which began in 1988 to study the feasibility of incorporating trade division concepts from other unions into the structure of the Federation. This committee, working with AFL-CIO adviser Bill

Roehl, made a number of recommendations about the future of the Federation that the IEB adopted in 1990.

One key element of this "Roehl Report" was the creation of the Symphonic Services and Electronic Media Services Divisions, which now operate under the guidance of steering committees chosen from

David Ewart, RMA Executive Publisher

the rank-and-file members working in those particular areas. A second was the conversion of the "Summit Committee" – which consisted of representatives of the four player conferences, RMA, ICSOM, ROPA and OCSM – into the Player Conference Council consisting of the chief officers of each of the conferences, now with "formalized direct access to the IEB."

In Orlando, meanwhile, another chapter of RMA was formed, in part as a pre-emptive strike in case the major studios decided to shift film and TV scoring to Florida from southern California. In 1988, several of the majors (notably Disney and Universal) were building studios in central Florida. Suppose they decided to build scoring stages too?

At the time, violinist David Ewart was assistant concertmaster of the Orlando-based Florida Symphony Orchestra; he was also a delegate to ICSOM. Contacted by L.A. RMA vice president Sheldon Sanov, Ewart agreed to help by forming an RMA chapter. Within a year, he was president and the chapter had attracted more than 100 members.

As a chapter president, Ewart was invited to participate in the 1990 film negotiations. As it happened, a year-long strike destroyed the Florida Symphony and the apparent threat of scoring in Florida effectively disappeared. Ewart moved to Los Angeles in 1990 and became an L.A. RMA board member in 1991. He began editing the newsletter and was later named Executive Publisher, in charge of all newsletters, advertising, directories and public relations efforts for the organization.

RMA continued to grow in membership and financial health during this time. Bassist Neil Stubenhaus spearheaded the drive in Los Angeles for new members and higher dues throughout the late '80s and early '90s.

Stubenhaus felt a large membership and strong financial base could generate the respect that RMA needed to properly function

Neil Stubenhaus

within the AFM. His push for raising the dues met with resistance from his fellow board members, however; a jump from $45 to $75 in 1990 passed the RMA board by only one vote.

Writing solicitation letters, chairing annual membership drives and constantly pushing for more income, Stubenhaus created a tiered structure that was designed to encourage larger donations by those musicians who could comfortably afford the higher levels (contributing, sustaining, patron). The new plan generated nearly $50,000 in a matter of weeks during the first part of 1990.

By the time Stubenhaus resigned from the board in 1992, the Los Angeles chapter membership had grown to 700. Ewart succeeded Stubenhaus in this effort, significantly expanding the ranks to more than 1,000. (Stubenhaus and Ewart also expanded the L.A. membership directory into a massive and respected industry sourcebook.) The International RMA has a total membership of 2,500, including the vast majority of the estimated 3,000 professional recording musicians in the U.S. and Canada.

The status and power of the RMA became clear at the 1993 AFM convention, when the IEB had proposed a 2.5 percent work-dues assessment on royalties from both the film/TV and records Special Payments Funds. If approved, this tax – which was designed to help bail out the financially troubled Federation – would have cost SPF-eligible musicians an estimated $600,000.

At a Local 47 meeting attended by hundreds of recording musicians, "the members made it explicitly clear that any attack on the Funds would result in an overwhelming negative backlash against the Federation," according to a report in the April 1993 RMA newsletter. At the June AFM convention, a compromise was worked out that denied the AFM a piece of the musicians' royalties but did call for an additional 1/2 percent work dues (to be spent on the Electronic Media Services Division) and a new 12 percent work-dues formula for "new use" areas, among other provisions. In return, the AFM guaranteed the RMA participation in new SPF oversight committees, input on future Pension Fund trustee appointments, a look into reclassifying Special Payments as a "royalty fund," and involvement in a new advisory committee that also included the five major locals.

Later in 1993, the IEB appointed Dreith, Electronic Media Services Division head Dick Gabriel, and AFM President Mark Tully

Alan Wood, first AFM Vice President from Canada, 1965-1991

Massagli to the AFM half of the "oversight" committees for both the Motion Picture and Phonograph Special Payments Funds. At that time, projected 1994 collections were $30 million in the film SPF and $12 in the phono SPF, and those administering the funds were not being monitored in any formal way.

The committee was formed to "review and make recommendations as to the administrative expenses as well as the overall operation and performance of the funds."

As 1994 dawned, RMA again became an international organization with the revival of the long-dormant Toronto chapter. The original Toronto RMA, spearheaded by Graham Howes, Glenn Morley and Jack Zaza, was "more of an advisory committee than an organization," according to violist and current President Douglas Perry. "Interest in the group, while enthusiastic, never reached its potential and with the closing of tax breaks, the advent of MIDI and the change in economics of the music industry in general, the RMA lay dormant for the next ten years."

Alan Wood, former president of the Toronto local and vice president for Canada of the AFM, opened the Canadian AFM office in 1980 and maintained a strong relationship with recording musicians until his retirement in 1991. His departure and a poorly negotiated Canadian jingle agreement in 1993 gave rise to the new Toronto chapter.

"The level of discontent with the way the union [in Canada] was running our affairs, both in the local and within the Federation, boiled over into action with this final indignity," Perry said. Under the leadership of Brian Leonard and Steve Webster, the group gained official recognition from the AFM and the Canadian government.

"Though the primary focus in 1993 was on the jingle agreement, it became clear that the problems we faced were institutionally entrenched," Perry said. Through the efforts of the RMA Toronto,

Local 149's structure was redefined and a new slate of officers, nearly all RMA members, was elected. The RMA became involved with the Canadian Broadcasting Corporation radio/TV and jingle negotiations and was instrumental in choosing the new recording representative for the local, as well as advocating a Canadian TV Film agreement.

The following year was doubly significant for the RMA. It helped to strengthen ties between the AFM Player Conferences, and RMA President Dennis Dreith addressed a Congressional subcommittee on a topic of importance to musicians nationwide.

At the centennial-celebration AFM convention in June 1995, RMA joined with the other conferences on key legislation issues (including the move to name a rank-and-file player as a Pension Fund Trustee, with RMA veteran Dave Schwartz later named that individual).

Dreith testified at a hearing held June 28, 1995, before the House Judiciary Committee's Subcommittee on Intellectual Property and Judicial Administration. The topic was the proposed Digital Performance Right in Sound Recordings Act of 1995, which passed both houses of Congress and was signed by President Clinton later that year. The RMA president stressed the importance of a public performance right for musicians and songwriters with respect to digital transmissions.

FOR THE RECORD

John Williams at The Lost World: Jurassic Park *scoring session*

"Since the Golden Age of the great musicals down to the present day, the contribution of Hollywood's soundtrack recording musicians has been colossal.

"In the world of cinema these "behind the scenes" artists have set the universal standard for many years and are certain to continue their leadership role in this field for decades to come.

"They are truly among the greatest contributors to our country's artistic life and they are a cherished resource in which we can all take great pride."

— John Williams

FOR THE RECORD

THE RMA TODAY

The music business has undergone remarkable, even unforseeable changes in the past thirty years. Recording musicians originally banded together for an undeniably negative reason: the American Federation of Musicians had failed to keep up, to meet the needs of the new media, to adapt its old ways to properly service its professional members.

That's why the frustrated members of the Musicians Guild of America broke away. It took three contentious years of dual unionism to make the AFM wake up. And those years took their toll. Cecil Read – who is now a legend among Hollywood musicians – gave up playing and took a low-paying administrative job at Local 47. (*Variety* didn't even bother to print his 1987 obituary.) Lifelong friendships broke up over the Guild. People playing the same dates stopped speaking to each other.

Federation officials were forced to change their attitudes toward recorded music and those who made it, and made much-needed improvements in AFM agreements. Yet, in a just a few years, owing to long-entrenched policies, old-fashioned union politics and complex circumstances in both New York and Los Angeles, recording musicians once again were left out of the picture. Union leaders were negotiating terrible agreements out of sheer ignorance, and musicians were suffering both personally and professionally.

That's why the Recording Musicians Association was born. From humble, informal beginnings in New York, it has grown into an international organization of both respect and power within the music business and its own labor union.

Bassist Neil Stubenhaus candidly sums it up: "One of the main functions of the RMA is to assist the union in our negotiations for all of the contracts – because when we were not involved, they were ruining our contracts. They were giving away pieces of the contracts that could never be re-established: the jingle business, the record business, the film business, all of them. Getting them to respect us has been a slow process."

Dick Gabriel, who opened the AFM's Electronic Media Services Division office in Los Angeles in 1980 and now serves as assistant

Dick Gabriel

to the AFM president, believes the RMA is the best way for the Federation to get a quick reading on any issue affecting recording musicians.

"The most effective way I can get the input of the rank and file is through the RMA, because they're talking to each other all the time. It's an organization that communicates well within itself," he said.

(L to R) Local 47 President Bill Peterson, John Williams and Steven Spielberg

Noted Local 47 President Bill Peterson: "The needs and demands on a studio musician are different from those of a nightclub, casual or theater musician." While past relations with the locals have been stormy, things are very different with the RMA today, Peterson said. "We work together. It's very close and friendly. We understand that we need each other and we can work together for the benefit of all musicians."

FOR THE RECORD

Steve Young became president of the AFM in 1995. Unlike most of his predecessors, Young was not only a professional musician but also one who had been active in the recording field in Boston. Said Young: "The RMA has evolved over the years to become an important Player Conference within the American Federation of Musicians. It provides valuable input for the negotiating process

Steve Young, International AFM President 1995-

and monitoring of the contracts that we have. Anything we can do to get better agreements, and monitor those agreements, is to the benefit of all of us.

"It's important," he added, "that the International Executive Board be better informed, and the RMA has been working hard to educate the AFM in all aspects of recorded music. The RMA provides a pulse on how the musicians feel about the agreements they work under.

"The attitude [toward recording musicians] has changed drastically over the decades. They're extremely important. I believe they are the best musicians in the world for recording. They're an important asset to the coalition-building that we've been doing over the years within the union. They have become an integral part of that process, as they should have been all along."

Over the past decade, RMA President Dennis Dreith has become a knowledgable and respected negotiator whose presence at AFM contract talks is welcomed. (A far cry from the 1983 jingle negotiations, when AFM President Victor Fuentealba's first words to a well-informed but less seasoned Dreith were, "Shut up, Dennis.")

"He understands how the war is fought in the trenches," says Harold Bradley, veteran Nashville guitarist and currently president of AFM Local 257. "Without his input, and that of other RMA members, we would be in serious trouble. During my time in office, the AFM has really embraced the RMA and asked their input on everything, because they represent the players." (With his brother Owen, Bradley built the first recording studio on Nashville's now famous Music Row in 1954. A recording musician since 1946, he has supported Nashville-RMA presence at negotiating sessions since he became president of 257 in 1990.)

The road hasn't always been smooth. One of Dreith's most memorable encounters with a high-powered Federation official oc-

Harold Bradley (right), President Local 257, Nashville, with Chet Atkins, 1991

curred in early 1988, after the RMA had achieved conference status and a seat at the negotiating table. It involved the famous Henry Kaiser, who had been counsel to every AFM president dating back to James C. Petrillo.

Then-AFM President Marty Emerson wanted to retain Kaiser for the upcoming contract negotiations. But, recalled Chase Craig (then a trustee of Local 47), "There was a very strong push to retire Henry Kaiser. A number of people had labeled him 'the magnificent dinosaur.' He was a marvelous man, very intelligent, who had gone past his prime."

To the leadership of the RMA at the time, Henry Kaiser represented the past. He had opposed the Guild and he was not thought of as a progressive attorney. Dreith attended the IEB meeting in Fort Myers, Florida, to explain the RMA's position.

"Henry was there," Dreith remembered. "Here was a guy who had appeared before the Supreme Court and had been counsel to Presidents and ambassadors and industry giants and Federation leaders."

With Kaiser at the table, Dreith made his pitch to Emerson and the IEB: "With all due respect to Mr. Kaiser, it is the position of the RMA that it would not be our choice to have Mr. Kaiser negotiate for us. We prefer a negotiator of our own choosing."

Kaiser, in one fell swoop, grabbed his cigar, smashed it down on the table and said, in a great booming voice, "What did you say? Who do you think you are?!" Kaiser was fuming – yet he invited Dreith to dinner that night. "He was an amazing intellectual and an amazing bully all at the same time," Dreith said. "And, I came to realize, a very complex man."

Over drinks that evening, the two men became acquainted, and Dreith was both praised and enlightened by the legendary Henry Kaiser. "You know, kid, you've got [guts]," he said. "I'll say that much for you. I like a guy with [guts]. You weren't afraid to stand

George Cohen, AFM General Counsel

up to me. But you know you're not going to win this fight. You know what your problem is? You don't know how to negotiate. You come in here, you've got one position, and it's a loser. You've got nowhere else to go. You should have done your homework. Marty wants me; he's the boss. You've got a lot to learn about how this game is played. There must be something else you guys want. Maybe you ought to think about it."

Weeks later, at a meeting with Emerson, Dreith asked for, and got, that "something else": a seat on the negotiating subcommittee with full voting rights.

Henry Kaiser never did negotiate another contract. He was diagnosed with cancer and died a few months later. If the circumstances had been different, Dreith reflected, "Henry and I would have had some stimulating debates, but I think we would have been friends. In that short time, he did teach me something very valuable that really set us on the path."

George Cohen, a senior partner in Kaiser's Washington law firm, succeeded Kaiser as General Counsel for the AFM. (Cohen also negotiates on behalf of baseball's Major League Players Association, the National Basketball Players Association, and several airline pilots associations.) He has served as the Federation's chief negotiator for 10 years and noted that, during that period, AFM presidents Emerson, Massagli and Young "have expanded the role which RMA representatives have played on the negotiating committee.

"In most of those negotiations, RMA President Dennis Dreith has served as a player-representative member of the negotiating

Dennis Dreith asks for a vote on a resolution

committee, and in that capacity, Dennis has been an invaluable resource to the entire committee, both in the internal planning and strategizing and during the course of the negotiating process itself.

"Thereafter, once the industry-wide agreements have been reached, Dennis has contributed mightily to the Federation staff and counsel in making sure that the agreements were administered and enforced, so as to fully protect the contractual rights of the recording musicians whom the Federation represents."

Even Victor Fuentealba, who had his ups and downs with the RMA during his sometimes-stormy tenure as AFM president, agrees that the RMA has been good for recording musicians. "I think that any organization that is formed to better conditions for its members does good. The only obvious drawback is, when you have a lot of subsidiary groups within your organization, you can't move as quickly as sometimes as effectively with decisions as you could in the past, because you have to run things by these subsidiary organizations.

"But, on the whole, they have contributed a great deal, particularly when you come to negotiations," Fuentealba continued. "You have representatives who have talked to the players and who have worked with the players. They're on the grassroots level. They see what's happening at the sessions and they know where the problems are.

"The RMA has grown through the years and is accepted by the recording musicians. I would say they do an excellent job of conveying the issues of their members to the Federation."

In fact, points out Los Angeles RMA board member David Ewart, the RMA also contributes enormously to the financial health of the Federation. "Together, the symphonic musicians and the recording musicians – the professional players who make up only a fraction of the total AFM membership of 118,000 – pay a large portion of the Federation's bills. In addition, player conferences like ICSOM and RMA are important political organizations. They represent and fulfill the need for self-determination."

Without RMA, Treasurer Tony Cooke believes, "there would be no union recording. It would have been negotiated away. The producers would have destroyed the recording business.

Tony Cooke, International RMA Treasurer

"The RMA is at an important time," he adds. "It's come of age within the AFM now. The question is, where do we go from here? We've got a problem with an ailing AFM. Can we find a way to help it stay alive? Or are we going to be literally driven out, to go it alone, which poses all kinds of new problems?"

An equally important challenge for the future combines both business and musical concerns. "We've become very well promoted in recent years," Cooke notes. "The presence and visibility is now an entirely different picture from five years ago. We need to not lose sight of the fact that we have a role to play now that we've got their attention: convincing employers that we are the people they need.

"You've got to do more than just put an ad out. You've got to also find ways to let them know that it's practical to work here. They don't have to go to London or Salt Lake City. There are ways that can work within our contracts that are affordable."

And, says Cooke, "We need to not lose sight of the quality of what we do as players. So that when people do come to us, having been attracted by our publicity and promotion, we deliver the product that they expect, and in fact do better than that."

Today, the RMA continues to expand in scope, becoming active not only in Washington politics – regularly meeting with members of Congress on issues pertaining to recording musicians – but also on the international scene (recently establishing a "cultural and informational free-trade agreement" with the Musicians Rights Commission of Japan, for example).

It has taken decades of struggle. But musicians performing in recording studios across the United States and Canada have at last achieved, against very long odds and at times surprisingly vehement opposition from within their own union, what all workers want and should have: to be properly compensated for their skills and to have a voice in their own destiny.

Randy Newman plays for "RMA Nite IV," August 3, 1996

FOR THE RECORD

Dennis Dreith (L) and Bill Peterson

"While past relations have been stormy, things are very different today...we understand that we need each other and we can work together for the benefit of all musicans."

— *Bill Peterson, Local 47 President*

BIBLIOGRAPHY AND A NOTE ON SOURCES

More than three dozen first-person interviews were the backbone of this book. All quotations, except for those books and published articles cited below and union literature cited in the text itself, were drawn from interviews done by the author during the first five months of 1997.

Whenever possible, the information gleaned from interviews was double-checked against other sources. Only a handful of books have covered some of the issues discussed here, and then not always reliably. That meant considerable additional research involving the consumer press, trade press, labor press, and the files of the Recording Musicians Association itself (including all of the minutes of board and membership meetings and RMA correspondence).

RMA newsletters and Local 47 campaign material were helpful and informative, but many of the details about dates, locations and issues discussed were provided by Jay Berliner, former RMA officer in New York. His extensive files, copious notes on negotiations and thorough record-keeping were invaluable to the chronology.

A major part of the research involved consulting dozens of contemporaneous accounts of these events as reported in *Daily Variety, The Hollywood Reporter, The New York Times, The Los Angeles Times, Los Angeles Mirror-News, Los Angeles Herald-Express, Saturday Review* and *Weekly Variety*, dating back as far as the early 1950s. Back issues of *Overture* (the official publication of Local 47) were also extensively consulted.

"The American Federation of Musicians: Celebrating Our Centennial" in *International Musician*, October 1996.

Berliner, Jay. "United We Stand, Divided We Fall: An RMA History Lesson" in *International Musician*, January 1992.

Carpenter, Willard. "Rebellion in Local 47," in *Frontier*, April 1956.

"James Caesar Petrillo" in *Current Biography*, 1940.

Kraft, James P. *Stage to Studio: Musicians and the Sound Revolution, 1890-1950.* Baltimore: Johns Hopkins University Press, 1996.

Leiter, Robert D. *The Musicians and Petrillo.* New York: Bookman Associates Inc., 1953.

Nash, Ted. "The Musicians Guild of America." Unpublished commentary, September 1996.

Poe, Elizabeth. "Revolt Against Petrillo" in *The Nation*, May 5, 1956.

Read, Cecil F. "Report on Trust Fund Appeal," in *Overture*, April 1956.

Rothstein, Murray. "The Musicians Guild of America: History of a Membership Revolt" in *Allegro*, September 1996.

Sanjek, Russell, and David Sanjek. *American Popular Music Business in the 20th Century.* New York: Oxford University Press, 1991.

Seltzer, George. *Music Matters: The Performer and the American Federation of Musicians.* Metuchen, N.J.: Scarecrow Press, Inc., 1989.

Velie, Lester. "The Union That Fights Its Workers" in *Readers Digest*, December 1956.

ABOUT THE AUTHOR

Jon Burlingame is the nation's leading writer on music for motion pictures and television. His first book, *TV's Biggest Hits: The Story of Television Themes from "Dragnet" to "Friends"* – a history of American television scoring – was published in 1996 to widespread critical praise in both the mainstream and music press.

A professional journalist since 1973, he has written about film and TV music for such publications as *Premiere* and *Emmy* magazines, *The Washington Post, New York Newsday* and the *New York Daily News*. He teaches film-music history at the University of Southern California and, over the past five years, has served as moderator or speaker on several panels at

international film-music conferences in New York, Los Angeles, and Switzerland.

Burlingame is a frequent contributor to *The Hollywood Reporter* on current topics dealing with music for movies and television. He has also written the liner notes for albums by such esteemed film composers as John Williams, Henry Mancini, Jerry Goldsmith, John Barry, Lalo Schifrin, Michel Legrand, Bernard Herrmann, David Raksin and Ennio Morricone.

He recently wrote and co-produced "Jerome Moross: American Original," a short documentary film on the life and career of the film composer responsible for such classic Americana scores as *The Big Country*. In June 1996, he wrote, co-produced and hosted "Fifty Years of Television Music," a two-hour show at the Academy of Television Arts & Sciences (North Hollywood, Calif.) that combined classic clips with live performances (both vocal and big-band) of favorite television themes.

Burlingame began his career writing for upstate New York daily newspapers. He worked for eight years as a film critic and began writing about television on a full-time basis in 1984, spending more than six years as the daily TV critic for the New York-based United Feature Syndicate, a Scripps-Howard company.

He is currently at work on his third book, *The Newmans of Hollywood*, which will chronicle the lives and careers of the several members of the Newman family who were, and continue to be, highly influential in the world of American film music.